ESALEN

COOKBOOK

ESALEN
COOKBOOK

Healthy and Organic Recipes from Big Sur

Charlie Cascio

Gibbs Smith, Publisher
Salt Lake City

First Edition
10 09 08 07 06   5 4 3 2 1

Text © 2006 Charlie Cascio

Photography © 2006 Joyce Oudkerk Pool on pages 3, 4, 7, 11, 13, 14, 20, 21, 26, 31, 32, 34, 37, 42, 44, 50, 53, 54, 57, 60, 64, 67, 68, 74, 76, 78, 79, 80, 83, 85, 86, 87, 88, 94, 99, 100, 104, 108, 110, 111, 114, 118, 121, 128, 132, 133, 135, 136, 137, 143, 144, 154, 157, 161, 167, 168, 171, 182, 184, 188, 191, 194, 197, 198

Photography by Daniel Bianchetta (www.bigsurphoto.com) © 2006 Esalen Institute on pages 2, 6, 7, 10, 12, 16, 17, 18, 21, 28, 30, 48, 72, 97, 98, 120, 142, 158, 192, 196, 200

All rights reserved. No part of this book may be reproduced by any means whatsoever without written permission from the publisher, except brief portions quoted for purpose of review.

Esalen is a registered trademark of Esalen Institute.

Published by
Gibbs Smith, Publisher
P.O. Box 667
Layton, Utah 84041

Orders: 1.800.748.5439
www.gibbs-smith.com

Designed by Sheryl Dickert Smith
Food Styling by Nani Steele
Printed and bound in Hong Kong

Library of Congress Cataloging-in-Publication Data
Cascio, Charlie.
   Esalen cookbook / Charlie Cascio ; photographs by Joyce Oudkerk Pool.—
1st ed.
   p. cm.
   ISBN 1-58685-852-1
1. Cookery. 2. Esalen Institute. I. Title.

TX714.C3763 2006
641.5—dc22   2006005452

CONTENTS

FOREWORD

ESALEN: THE MAGIC AND THE DREAM

Esalen. The very word conjures magic for many thousands of students and seekers who come here each year, the hundreds of teachers and residential staff who live or spend time in this timeless spot, where the foothills of the Ventana Range fall sharply to the Pacific Ocean. Parts of these grounds were sacred to the Esselen Indians, from whom the Institute takes its name. They believed the spot was an energy confluence of all the waters—deep earth, mountain, sky, and sea. Many say that they think and feel more deeply at Esalen, that conversations on Esalen's healing grounds, in the classrooms and the lodge, or down at the mineral baths by the swelling surf are more alive, more intense, and more whole and fresh than conversations they have in other places.

People come in search of that wholeness. From its beginnings, Esalen's founders insisted on their commitment to reowning our whole human potential in the deepest sense—spirit and body, shadow and light, self and our shared community. To the inquiries of the mind would be added the language of the body, the struggles of the heart, the yearnings of the spirit, and the full expression of our social nature, our relational world. To each of these dimensions of our nature they would bring the light of conscious awareness, the darkness of mystery, and the energy of committed dialogue.

And more than this: true wholeness means the interplay and complex union of all these dimensions of human experience together, the full human potential for integration of being. Thus Esalen's themes have been not just body but mind/body, not just spirit but body/spirit, the mindful heart and the heartful mind, spiritual activism through political initiatives, and all the other combinations and unities we might explore that bring us toward that wholeness.

All this goes on at Esalen, bringing a steady stream of the most stimulating students and teachers from around the world—to learn, restore, relax, expand, heal, and then take that expanded capacity out into the world again, with renewed commitment for the journey.

At the center of it all, physically and psychically, are the gardens, lavish and yet with a homey touch, hand-tended and natural, richly ornamental and yet highly productive at the same time. These gardens, together with the farm at the north end of the campus, supply a large portion of the foodstuffs that go into the amazing Esalen kitchen each day and come back out in the form of hundreds of individual meals, scores of platters, trays, tureens, and serving pans that nourish and delight us here at Esalen each and every day of the year.

How do they do it? "Teamwork," they may say with a shrug when you ask them, and then admit that they sometimes ask themselves that same question. The entire operation is a testimony to the integration of incongruities that has always been Esalen's hallmark: a core staff of highly dedicated and talented individuals, inspiring and energizing a diverse student crew from around the world. They create meals in a small and crowded workspace, yet with the highest standards of cleanliness and the unexpected efficiencies smallness can sometimes bring. They offer a menu that changes with the seasons and with the actual day's harvest. At mealtime the serving stations are loaded, varied, and enticing, and always there is the nourishing array of Esalen organic breads, fresh-baked and available all day (and all night) long.

I suspect part of the answer to how they do it is sheer magic—but a magic each of us can share. At its heart is the alchemy of *shared intention and spirit*, which after all is what is taught here at Esalen, in the end. Students, interns, staff, guest workers—everybody at Esalen is a seeker in his or her own way; everybody is on a path with its own explorations, challenges, joys, distractions, processes. Our intentions are as varied as our individual psyches and journeys; and our intention and our shared journey are one.

And then out of this magic, this intoxicating mix of earth, mind, heart, spirit, and community, three times a day, three hundred sixty-five days a year (and one more on leap year), the mealtime show goes on. Each and every day some contribution comes in from the farm and gardens, to be included in the meal. Three times each day the kitchen staff blesses the meal on time, and nourishing food goes out—a staggering total of some 250,000 variously loaded plates a year, with always a veggie choice, always a vegan alternative in the kitchen, and almost always a meat or fish alternative as well.

And isn't all that, on a smaller scale, the challenge many of us face in our own kitchens: how to render routine, pressures of time and space, and the challenge of "whatever we've got on hand" into the magic of nourishment, blessing, and the deep restoration of body and heart that an *intentional meal* provides to the human spirit?.

You'll find that magic in the pages of this handsome book, in the wonderful recipes developed and adapted for home proportions by Charlie Cascio, longtime Chief Resident Magician of the Esalen Kitchen, together with his fellow magicians and crew. You'll find it too in the stunning food photography of Joyce Oudkerk Pool and the food styling of Nani Steele. It's also in the beautiful photos of the Esalen grounds and of the staff and students by Daniel Bianchetta. And you'll find it in your own kitchen when you let yourself be inspired by these images, these recipes, and all the wealth of spirit and experience that go into them.

If you've never been to Esalen, travel here in these pages, feel a bit of the energy so many feel, and take that inspiration and intention into your own home and life. Then follow it up with a visit to us with your whole person when you can—restore your body and spirit in the courses, the baths, the lodge at mealtimes, the gardens and grounds. And again, take that inspiration and intention into your own life.

If you've been here before, perhaps many times, come back soon and whenever you can. In the meantime, take this book as a talisman to retrigger that special state of being, that magic, till you can be here in person again. Use it as a reminder that all of us are alchemists, all of us are potential magicians, really—in our kitchens and in our lives. All of us are on a journey, and every day we take whatever is at hand—out of the challenges and the needs and the bounty our shared earth provides—and render it into the most nourishing service we can, as creatively and gratefully as we can, for others and for ourselves. Remembering that is the greatest gift and in a way the whole point of Esalen.

Enjoy, transform, serve.

With blessings for your journey,
Gordon Wheeler
President, Esalen Institute

ACKNOWLEDGMENTS

I offer a most grateful thank you to all of the great people of the Esalen kitchen who worked so hard with such large volumes, to create and to master these and many more recipes during their daily routine of feeding the masses in the dining lodge.

I would like to give my appreciation to these folks who gave me their culinary support, encouragement, and physical help to make this book possible: Robin Burnside, Angela Karegeannes, Jaelitza, Denise Ladwig, Rachel Fann, John Blunt, Bill Herr, Liam McDermott, Flanagan Mackenzie, and most of all my charming wife, Marion, who supported and helped me throughout the recipe testing and writing of this book.

I would like to thank David Price for his supervision over this project.

I would like to thank Dick Price, who inspired me to create a compassionate kitchen, to believe in my fellow man and woman, and to give them a chance to go beyond the limits of their boundaries.

ABOUT THE ESALEN KITCHEN

The Esalen kitchen serves 750 meals a day. We are open 360 days each year and provide organic, wholesome, world-class food to our staff, to our community, and to people who come each week to experience our workshops and participate in other activities. Fifty percent of the vegetables served by the Esalen kitchen are grown on the Esalen organic farm and are fresh-picked hours before they are consumed.

The Esalen kitchen is comprised of a small full-time staff, with the balance of the kitchen family made up of both short- and longer-term "work scholars," who come here to participate in a 28-day workshop. In return, they work in our unique kitchen environment to pay for their tuition. The Esalen kitchen is, indeed, unique: it is a professional commercial kitchen just by the volume it serves, and it is a teaching kitchen due to the fact that three-fourths of the staff is comprised of nonprofessional, transient employees. The Esalen kitchen is also a personal growth kitchen, where workers can express their own uniqueness. Each day, time is taken in the flow of preparing 750 meals to listen to each other's thoughts, questions, points of view, and personal feelings and emotions. This builds compassion, understanding, dedication, and caring between the kitchen workers. Employees care profoundly about giving their best when they are acknowledged as humans. All of these traits are kneaded into the meals we serve our guests and staff.

Many chefs are amazed at how we accomplish such a feat. We at Esalen developed a method of management I call the "compassionate kitchen." It empowers all employees who come through the kitchen doors with confidence to produce their best, go beyond their boundaries, and express any and all of their culinary dreams. After thirty-five years of culinary experience—traversing many different aspects of the art of preparing, cooking, and serving food—I've

realized how *not* to run a kitchen. Most kitchens are not very friendly places and run in a very military fashion. Employees are told to do as ordered in an "all work and no fun" environment. These kitchens are boiling over with high stress as thoughts of anger, fear, and apathy fill the employees and marinate into the food that they prepare at breakneck speed to meet a never-ending stream of deadlines (for breakfast, lunch, and dinner), with no time to honor the individual employee. At Esalen, we transformed the hard work and turned it into fun. We also put a value on clear communication, honoring each individual's uniqueness, taking risks by believing in people, giving them positive feedback when they do a good job, and having an understanding ear when mistakes are made. Employee morale and creativity are high in this type of environment and the end result is found in the food.

Food makes it possible for us to do everything we do; it gives us energy for physical activities as well as non-physical activities such as talking, thinking, and feeling. Food can be for some of us the only contact we have with nature. A relationship exists between what we eat and the way we feel, yet many people see no connection between what they consume in the way of food and the state of their mental, physical, and spiritual health. Food preparation is the art of transforming many levels of energy into a form that the body and soul can digest and assimilate. Beautifully prepared food is one of the most basic and satisfying pleasures of life.

The most important and most overlooked ingredient in any recipe is the preparer of that recipe. Yes, that's right—the cook. Concrete ingredients such as the freshest fruits, herbs, and vegetables are important in any recipe, of course; but the attitude of the cook, the subtle messages and energies that are incorporated into the recipe in the process of preparation, is never given any credible thought, though it should be. A certain positive awareness in the cook's attitude will almost secure success in the kitchen. A stressful, insecure, angry, or fearful attitude on the part of the cook will impart these feelings into the food and ultimately be absorbed by whoever eats it. Those of you who were fortunate to have a mother who is a great cook know what I'm talking about when I say that every dish that mamma made was great—great because of the incredible effort and care, the loving tenderness that she had when she prepared food for her family. Preparing food with a warm heart is a direct expression of love.

When I took over the Esalen kitchen eight years ago, I had a strong commitment to the belief that the individual can help to change the world by action. I was eager to create the idea of a "compassionate kitchen." I wanted to bring the humane view into the realm of kitchen management, to create a kitchen culture that would reflect a good morale, mentally and physically healthy employees, flowing creativity, high productivity, great food, and fun in preparing that food. I used the philosophy of Dick Price, Esalen cofounder, for my recipe to this new approach to kitchen management. This was to allow people to express themselves and to witness that expression without judg-ment. Taking risks, believing in people, and empowering them with confidence to believe in themselves is the key to the magical success of the Esalen kitchen.

By empowering these untrained, unprofessional students with confidence that they could produce healthy, world-class food, by giving them a guiding hand with culinary technique, and by allowing them the chance to express their creativity, the Esalen kitchen became not just a place to prepare food but a loose-fitted family with high values, caring feelings, concern, and understanding for each other. We blossomed into an interdependent kitchen working with one goal: to present the best meals from our hearts to our guests and our community.

So, welcome to the Esalen kitchen. This cookbook is a collection of recipes from the past forty years that this kitchen has served to its guests and community. It is imbued with the creativity that has passed through the kitchen doors during that time. All of the recipes have one magic ingredient in common. It's one you can't find on the shelf of your local super-market. It's the compassionate, warm heart of the people that make up the Esalen kitchen, their sincere caring about the food they prepare. The people—cooks, bakers, salad makers, and dishwashers—and the organic, compassionate love they put into the food they prepare is the magical ingredient of the Esalen kitchen and is what this book is about.

Esalen is very much like a small village, with about 250 people on its property at any given moment. The Esalen dining lodge and kitchen is the center of this village, somewhat like the village square or the town meeting hall. It is without a doubt the main source of physical and social nutrition at Esalen. The dining lodge is filled with long redwood tables, seating about twenty people to a table. Everyone eats with one another at Esalen. The buffet-style meals can be exciting because you never know who will be sitting next to you at mealtime. It could be a billionaire or someone who has saved up for two years to be able to participate in a weeklong seminar. An artist, massage therapist, corporate CEO, organic farmer, spiritual teacher, or a homemaker—people from Germany to India to Cleveland, Ohio—they all break bread and sip soup side-by-side. This eclectic mix of diners create a wonderful stew of conversation in the shadow of the Pacific Ocean. The dining lodge is open twenty-three hours a day, closing for one hour of cleaning at 7:00 a.m.

Outside of mealtimes, organic breads (fresh from our bakery) and hot and cold drinks are available in the dining lodge. At anytime of the night or day you may find small groups of people in deep conversation, someone writing a letter or reading a book, or two people who have just met and are starting up a lifelong friendship.

The dining lodge is the hub of social activity, and in one corner of this lodge is a pair of swinging doors that open into a world of a constantly moving energy. It's here where the hearth of Esalen is hidden. Here in the Esalen kitchen, where the transformation of raw ingredients into delicious-tasting, healthy nourishment takes place, for me is the heart and soul of Esalen itself.

As you walk through the big swinging doors in the corner of the dining lodge, you enter a world of constant activity. This kitchen, like many commercial kitchens, is brimming with sights and sounds that fill the space with activity. We have three deadlines in the Esalen kitchen—breakfast, lunch, and dinner—seven days a week. Because of these deadlines, we are constantly in motion from 7:00 in the morning to 10:00 at night.

The Esalen kitchen has a physical resemblance to many commercial high-volume kitchens. There is a large wooden worktable in the middle of the kitchen that can accommodate up to ten people preparing food. There is also a chef worktable that is beside the row of stoves, convection ovens, griddle, char broiler, pressure steamer, and wok burner. Racks of stainless steel pots and wooden cutting boards are neatly stacked at the end of this table. A salad-chef worktable and a dishwashing area round out the workspace; the walls are lined with more worktables and large sinks. Doors lead off this room

into large walk-in refrigerators, freezers, food pantry, and bakery.

This ordinary-looking workspace enables us to prepare hundreds of meals at a time and is also a cauldron for personal transformation. It's where raw, organic nourishment is transformed into flavorful meals by people who care about the quality of this transformation. The alchemy of transformation is the secret ingredient that fuels the magic of the Esalen kitchen. The fire that supports this change springs forth from the heat of the ovens, the steam of the pressure steamer, the flames of the char broiler, and the passionate hearts of the cooks who fill this commercial kitchen with their creativity and their compassion. And this is all simmered together with acceptance.

The Esalen kitchen's approach to food is accepting all of the food; we leave the skin on the potatoes and cook with unrefined ingredients. And we also accept the whole person in our employees—their anger and sadness as well as their joy and love. The kitchen celebrates the tears of its workers; whether they be tears of joy or tears of sadness, it's all "salt for the soup."

Esalen's kitchen has been, and still is, a great crossroads. It has offered, and will continue to offer, life-changing transformations to those who enter its space. It's a space where those who have always dreamed of being the best chef or baker in the world can live their dream. Where those who have lost themselves in the ever-involved world can become free of the prison of living the image of what others think they should be. I've seen in my tenure here United Nation directors become great dishwashers, heart surgeons become sourdough bread bakers, corporate consultants become pastry chefs, and federal prosecutors create new recipes for 250 people. People transforming themselves in the act of transforming food is the workshop of the Esalen kitchen. The meal is the physical transformation of the workers and their work. There is a sign over the door of the Esalen kitchen that proclaims: "Work Is Love Made Visible." Welcome to the Esalen kitchen.

NOTES ON COOKING

DEHYDRATED CANE JUICE

In this cookbook, I recommend using dehydrated cane juice rather than refined white sugar. Refined white sugar is bad for the body. Sucanat or dehydrated cane juice can be directly substituted for it. Sucanat is a natural sugar that contains the minerals and vitamins needed for your body to digest the sugar.

Refined white sugar is unnatural and unhealthy for the human body. It has absolutely no food value. In addition, it has been stripped of the alkaline minerals that are needed to digest sugar. Unrefined sweeteners have a natural balance of sugar and alkaline minerals. These types of sweeteners don't stress the body or upset its natural harmonious balance like refined sugars do. Refined sugars have a jolting impact on the stomach. The blood must maintain a neutral Ph balance. However, when you eat refined sugars, they immediately turn the blood Ph acidic. The body must strip alkaline minerals, especially calcium and iron, in order to balance the blood Ph. This stresses the pancreas to produce more insulin to regulate the blood sugar before the whole body is traumatized.

Refined sugar, no matter what color it is, will always be in a granulated "crystal" form. In commercial powdered sugar, the crystals have been ground; in commercial brown sugar, the crystals have been colored with molasses or caramel. If the sugar is in granulated crystal form, it's refined.

There is on the market natural, organic sugar that claims to be dehydrated cane juice. This is half true, because all refined sugar from sugar cane has had the water boiled out of it as one of the first steps of refining—at this point it is dehydrated cane juice. After that, however, the healthy minerals and vitamins are also refined out. These minerals and vitamins are instrumental in digesting and assimilating the sugar cane juice into the body. Don't be deceived by healthy-sounding names like "raw sugar," "cane sugar," "turbinado sugar," or "fructose sugar." They are all denatured, highly refined sugars and are just as unhealthy as refined white sugar. Fructose sugar is not from fruit as the name implies, but is made from highly refined corn syrup. Turbinado sugar gets its name from the process used to refine and denature the sugar. Raw sugar has had the bleaching process eliminated, but is also denatured. All these sugars are just as harmful to the body as the white refined variety.

Except when the author of an original Esalen recipe insisted that I use refined sugar, I have substituted evaporated cane juice for refined sugar throughout this book. Evaporated cane juice goes under the brand names of Sucanat and Rapunzel's Rapadura.

Back in the early '90s, I attended the BioFach Organic Trade Fair in Frankfurt, Germany. This is the largest organic trade fair in the world. Growers, manufacturers, and suppliers of organic food and cosmetics from all over the world gather in Frankfort every year to display their merchandise and to make contact with one another. I was in charge of a booth for a friend of mine who owned an organic bakery in France.

My neighbor in the booth next to me was representing the country of Bolivia, displaying organic quinoa, the grain of the ancient Incas. In the booth on the other side of me was a Brazilian company called Sucanat. I had studied the effects of refined sugar on the human body, and I was fascinated to discover that this product was pure sugar cane juice that has had the water evaporated out at low temperatures. All of the god-given minerals and vitamins that lived in the sugar cane at the time of juicing are there—no refining had taken place. This really was raw, unadulterated, unrefined, and unbleached sugar.

Sucanat has one advantage over other natural sweeteners. It can be substituted in recipes calling for white refined sugar on a one-to-one basis. Other natural unrefined sweeteners such as maple syrup or honey are in a liquid form, and the recipe must be changed to accommodate the extra liquid.

Dehydrated cane juice has a brown color and is in the form of uncrystallized granules. When you dilute dehydrated cane juice with water it tastes just like fresh-squeezed sugar cane juice. It has a pleasant mild flavor that balances and entices other flavors to come forward. I highly recommend incorporating this into your cooking.

COOKING OILS

Oil is a very important factor for health. In this cookbook, I have simply stated "vegetable oil" or "olive oil" in the recipes. It's important to use unrefined and naturally extracted oil for your salads and cooking needs.

Go into a modern American supermarket and all the vegetable oils on the shelf—except one—will have no color, no order, and no taste. All these oils have been super-refined, stripped of their nutrients, bleached, and deodorized. Most of the oils on your grocer's shelf have been extracted from the base seed or nut through the use of chemical solvents, which have destroyed the nutrients in the oil. This is why there is no taste, no smell, and no color in the oil. This type of oil is a source of nutrient-deficient calories, similar to sugar, but unlike sugar, the oils are loaded with indigestible toxins that the body will have to store, mostly as fat.

The only exception on the grocery shelf is extra-virgin cold-pressed olive oil. This is guaranteed unrefined oil and is the healthiest choice in the supermarket. And it will be the only oil on the shelf that has odor, taste, and color. At one point in their lives all the oils on the grocery shelf had these same qualities, but by industrial refining processes, manufacturers have destroyed their integrity.

In natural food stores you can find unrefined oils that still hold their integrity, but be sure they say "unrefined" on the label because a lot of natural food stores sell the same nutrient-deficient oils as your local supermarket. No matter how many natural, low-cholesterol, or other healthy-sounding messages are written on the bottle, if it is not marked "unrefined" on the front label of the bottle, it's been robbed of its nutrients.

If an oil isn't marked "expeller pressed," it means petrochemical solvents (probably heptane or hexane) have extracted the oil. They are used because they extract more oil from the source, and we are told that these petrochemicals are refined out of the oil after the extraction. It has never been definitively proven, however, that all the solvent is taken out of the oil. Even in minute amounts, these solvents are highly toxic.

I suggest you use organic extra-virgin olive oil in the dishes you prepare. It is a health-enriching oil that has been shown to be beneficial against cardio-vascular disease and cancer. It's a fairly stable oil and can handle light sautéing, up to 300 degrees F. If you need to use oil in a dish for which the taste of the olive oil will not complement the recipe's flavor, use an oil that is labeled "unrefined," "organic," and "expeller pressed." Organic, unrefined safflower, sunflower, sesame, and rice bran oil can be found in natural food stores. I suggest that you use these when olive oil is not appropriate. These four oils are fairly stable and can handle light sautéing. For high heat or deep frying, I would suggest using ghee (clarified butter) or coconut oil, since they have a high heat tolerance to molecular breakdown.

SOURDOUGH STARTER

If you want to bake sourdough bread and don't have a sourdough starter, you have three choices: (1) You can buy a dried sourdough culture, which can be found at your natural food store. (2) You can borrow a cup of starter from a friend (if you are lucky enough to have such a friend). Or (3), you can make the starter culture yourself. Believe it or not, making a sourdough culture is not rocket science. Here is an easy-to-follow recipe that will give you great results.

    2 teaspoons active dry yeast
    2 cups warm water
    2 cups whole wheat flour or rye flour

Mix the ingredients in a glass, plastic, or ceramic bowl using a wooden spoon. Don't use metal; it will react to the fermentation. Cover the bowl with a plate and leave at 65 to 70 degrees F (ambient room temperature) for 4 days or until small bubbles appear on the surface. The starter will smell like sourdough bread. Keep your starter in a glass or plastic jar or a ceramic crock and cover with a kitchen towel or loose-fitting lid.

If you use the starter every few days, it can stay at room temperature. If the starter is used less often, keep it in the fridge so its growth is slowed down. Try to keep at least 2 cups of starter active so you will always have a bit of old starter to replenish the culture. When you use the starter for baking, replenish the starter by stirring in the same volume that you have taken out, using equal parts flour and water.

STOCK-MAKING BASICS

All of the savory recipes in this book will taste good if you use water when they call for adding liquid. But to achieve excellent taste from soups and sauces, as well as from some of the lunch and dinner recipes, adding a stock base that you have made from fresh ingredients is the key.

Stocks are the basic foundation that flavor can build on. You make stocks by simmering meat trimmings, bones, vegetables, vegetable trimmings, and herbs in water. The first rule of stock making is to use fresh ingredients. Don't use ingredients that belong in the compost! Stocks are not a way to use up everything that you were going to throw out when you clean the fridge.

Chop the stock ingredients into small pieces; about 1 inch will do just fine. Quantity is not an issue with stock making; more ingredients bring out more flavor. Start your stocks with cold, fresh water and cook vegetable stocks a minimum of 1/2 hour and a maximum of 1 hour. Meat stocks should cook a minimum of 1 hour and poultry stocks a minimum of 2 hours.

Strain the ingredients out of the stock when you've finished cooking; this will eliminate any chance of the stock turning bitter. Certain vegetables should not be used for making stocks because they will turn a stock bitter. These include artichoke trimmings, bell peppers, all of the cabbage family (cabbage, cauliflower, broccoli, kale, Brussels sprouts, and kohl rabi), turnips, and red beets. Also do not use any spoiled vegetables, ground herbs, celery seed, or salt when making a stock.

A good recipe for a basic stock is 50 percent onions, 25 percent carrots, and 25 percent celery with some parsley, thyme, and bay leaf added to this mix. But remember, you don't have to follow a recipe to make a good stock.

A fresh stock base can be fortified by using a good-quality powdered soup and stock base. And if you don't have time to make a fresh stock, I can recommend two dehydrated stock bases: one is Vogue Cuisine (www.voguecuisine.com) and the other is Rapunzel Vegetable Broth (www.rapunzel.com). Both of these use fresh organic vegetables and are low in sodium. All the other brands I've tried are too salty and don't really have an interesting taste.

ORGANIC FRUITS AND VEGETABLES

Those of you who have been to Esalen may have noticed that the mashed potatoes or glazed carrots you were served in our dining lodge were prepared with their skins still intact. (Those small brown flecks you found in your mashed potatoes were not some exotic culinary herb from Esalen's organic garden, but potato skins.) The layer of cells just underneath the potato skin holds the richest concentration of minerals and vitamins the potato has to offer. According to J. Rodale in his book *The Complete Book of Food and Nutrition*, peeling potatoes results in a 47 percent loss of vitamin C. Since we at the Esalen kitchen are con-

cerned with offering food that has the highest amount of nutrition, you will almost always find potato skins and other skins of fruits and vegetables left on the food we serve. That's why you won't be asked to peel your vegetables in most of the recipes presented in this book

But hold on before you toss your vegetable peeler into the trash. The skin and the layer just under the skin of fruits and vegetables can also be a concentrated source of unhealthy residues of toxic agrichemicals. If you're going to follow Esalen's example of serving fruits and vegetables with the skin intact, then you must, and I stress must, also follow Esalen's example of being committed to using organic fruits and vegetables. At Esalen, we only use organic potatoes; that's why we offer them to our guests with their full nutritional value intact.

I strongly urge you to consider making a commitment to organically produced foods. I believe we would be a healthier society if mainstream America made a major transition to organic agriculture. Non-organic fruits and vegetables are almost always sprayed with toxic pesticides, and the plants get their nourishment from toxic chemical fertilizers that are put into the soil. Some produce is even dipped and coated with fungicides to prolong shelf life. Meat and dairy products are pumped full of hormones and chemicals. Their toxic residues are cumulatively stored in our bodies, and this accumulation causes our bodies to fall prey to degenerative diseases and premature aging.

We have all heard from experts and scientists that the amount of toxic chemical residue in non-organic foods is too little to affect our health. Their statistics are based on the toxic residue that's contained in one apple, for example. What they are not telling you is that when you eat that apple, the toxic residue you consume will never leave your body. The cumulative effect of eating many apples with toxic residue over a period of many years is what destroys our health. Also, it's a very dangerous endeavor to mix toxic chemicals, and yet this is exactly what we are doing when we eat different non-organic foods sprayed and fertilized with different chemicals.

Organic foods may be a little more expensive at the grocery store checkout stand, but they are less expensive than hospital and doctor bills from loss of our health. Eating organic foods is preventive medicine. And besides, organic foods taste so much better!

SEMOLINA FLOUR

Semolina flour is made from durum wheat, the hardest variety of wheat. It is too hard for most breads and is used almost exclusively as pasta flour. Semolina is a course grind of durum wheat and has a very high protein content.

THOMPSON RAISINS

Thompson grapes are the green, seedless grapes that you find all over America. They are also the most popular grape to dry into raisins. Yes, that's right—all those Sun-Maid Raisins that you have been eating are dried from Thompson grapes.

UNSULFURED APRICOTS

The process of sulfuring dried fruits, including apricots, is to maintain the bright color of the fruit. It also makes the fruit have a sour taste, kills all of the B vitamins, and gives one intestinal gas. Unsulfured apricots are darker than sulfured ones; they are also sweeter and healthier for you.

BREADS

Orange-Essence Raisin Bread | 28

Apricot Nut Bread | 30

Irish Soda Bread | 33

Banana Coconut Bread | 34

Company's Coming Scones | 35

Dark Russian Rye Bread | 36

Trustee Muffin | 37

Sourdough Rye Bread | 38

Spelt Sourdough Raisin Bread | 40

Honey Whole Wheat Bread | 41

Semolina Sourdough Bread | 43

ORANGE-ESSENCE RAISIN BREAD

Angela Karegeannes brought this recipe to the Esalen bakery. Soaking the raisins in orange extract water and using the soaking water in making the dough is the secret to this recipe's rich flavor. Try other extract flavors instead of orange, such as lemon or almond, to create new tastes.

Makes two 2-pound loaves

1	cup Thompson raisins (see page 25)
1	cup golden raisins
1	teaspoon orange extract
1¹/₂	cups warm water from the soaked raisins
5	teaspoons active dry yeast
1	tablespoon vanilla extract
4	tablespoons unsalted butter, melted
4	tablespoons sour cream
2	tablespoons dark brown sugar or Sucanat (dehydrated cane juice)
2	cups fine whole wheat flour
2	cups unbleached all-purpose flour

Angela Karegeannes

"I created this recipe during my first year in the bakery. I used to pull old cookbooks down from our dry storage pantry, and experiment with substitutions. I owe the idea of adding sour cream to a yeasted bread to the Tassajara Bread Book. Using orange extract–laden raisin water in the bread was, up until now, my secret to this recipe's rich flavor. I imagine many other extract flavors would do just as well. This bread is amazing as toast, with soft goat cheese and honey, or made into a bread pudding." —Angela Karegeannes

Place the raisins in a bowl and cover with almost-boiling water, and then add the orange extract. Stir. Let sit until raisins are plump but not too soft. Drain, reserving liquid. Set raisins aside.

Put 1¹/₂ cups of warm soaking liquid from the raisins in a mixing bowl and whisk in the yeast. Leave bowl in a warm, draft-free space for about 10 minutes to create a sponge-like texture on top. Whisk in the vanilla, butter, sour cream, sugar, and whole wheat flour to create a wet paste. Cover and let rest for 20 minutes in a warm, draft-free space.

Dust your hands with flour, and then knead 1¹/₄ cups of the unbleached flour into the dough. Knead for about 8 to 10 minutes or until the dough forms a soft ball and easily lifts off the sides of the bowl. Add the raisins and remaining unbleached flour and knead for another 8 to 10 minutes. The dough is ready when it is pliable and resilient and doesn't stick to your fingers when poked.

Shape dough into two equal rounds and let sit in a warm, draft-free space until doubled in size. Punch down the dough and reshape into two rounds. Let the dough raise again until doubled or when a finger poked into the dough barely springs back. Place on a baking sheet and bake in an oven preheated to 350 degrees F. Bake for 40 to 50 minutes or until the bread has a hollow sound when tapped on bottom. If you want to use a thermometer, the internal temperature should be 185 degrees F for doneness. Remove bread from oven and place on a wire cooling rack.

APRICOT NUT BREAD

This was a recipe that Flanagan Mackenzie brought to the Esalen bakery. Flanagan is a fiery Irish-Italian baker who would sit and knit socks during our weekly process meetings. She wrote, "I remember this recipe because it reminds me of the kids at Esalen—they would ask for it a lot. One afternoon Emilio, the 5-year-old son of our bookstore manager, came to the bakery and made a batch of this bread. He called it Butterfly and Bug Bread, and he did an amazing job!"

Makes 2 loaves

- 1¹/₂ cups dried unsulfured apricots (see page 25)
- 2 cups hot water
- 2 tablespoons unsalted butter
- 1 cup sugar
- 1 egg
- 3¹/₂ cups unbleached all-purpose flour
- 2 teaspoons non-aluminum baking powder
- 1 teaspoon baking soda
- ¹/₂ cup nonfat dry milk
- ¹/₂ cup fresh orange juice
- 1 cup chopped walnuts

Cut the apricots in 1/4-inch dice and cover with the hot water.

In a mixing bowl, cream the butter and sugar until you have a grainy paste. Add the egg and beat until you have a smooth mixture.

In another mixing bowl, sift the flour, baking powder, baking soda, and dry milk.

Pour the water off the soaking apricots and reserve 3/4 cup. Add orange juice. Whisk this liquid into the egg mixture. Stir this into the bowl with the dry ingredients, stopping when everything is incorporated. Gently fold the apricots and nuts into the dough. The dough should be the consistency of cake batter.

Oil 2 bread pans and divide the dough into them. Bake in a preheated oven at 350 degrees F for about 45 minutes or until a knife inserted into the bread comes out clean. The bread should have a golden brown appearance. Place on a wire rack to cool.

Emilio Eizner and Flanagan Mackenzie

Irish Soda Bread

IRISH SODA BREAD

This is an authentic recipe that was brought into our kitchen by Liam McDermott, an Irish American chef. He got it from his Irish grandmother, who brought it over with her from the Emerald Isle and adapted it for the Esalen kitchen. This loaf has a dense, scone-like texture and a rough, crunchy crust.

Makes 1 loaf

2	cups unbleached all-purpose flour
1¼	cups whole wheat pastry flour
1	cup rolled oats
1½	teaspoons baking soda
2	tablespoons Sucanat (evaporated cane juice) or brown sugar
1½	teaspoons cream of tartar
1	teaspoon sea salt
6	tablespoons unsalted butter
¾	cup plain yogurt
¾	cup buttermilk

In a 2-quart mixing bowl, sift and then mix the flours, oats, baking soda, Sucanat or brown sugar, cream of tartar, and salt.

Make sure the butter is cold and chop it into small pieces. Drop them into the mixing bowl and, with a pastry cutter or your fingers, work the butter into the mix until it will hold together when you squeeze a bit of flour in your hand.

Whisk the yogurt and buttermilk together and add to the mix. Mix until all the dry ingredients are absorbed and you have a biscuit-looking dough that is not sticky. If it is sticky, add a little more unbleached flour; if the dough is too dry and the flour is not being completely absorbed into the dough, add a small amount of water to pull it together.

Oil and flour a sheet pan, bread pan, or pie pan. You can shape the bread to accommodate the shape of the pan you want to use. Shape the dough into a round loaf if you are using the sheet or pie pan. Cut two cross slits in the bread and bake in a preheated oven at 350 degrees F for about 1 hour, or until a knife inserted into the bread comes out clean. Place on a rack to cool.

VARIATIONS

You can add nuts and dried fruit (such as raisins, apricots, or dried cranberries) to make a Fruit and Nut Soda Bread. Chocolate chips and coconut can also be added for a variation of this soda bread.

BANANA COCONUT BREAD

This is one of the sweet breads that comes out of our bakery and never lasts long on our bread bar. It is full of banana flavor and has a chewy coconut crumb texture. What a delight for those lucky guests who are lingering in the dining lodge when a baker brings out a hot loaf of this bread, filling the room with a banana-coconut aroma! This recipe was brought to Esalen by a cook who had a unique trait of singing her own style of opera in our walk-in freezer. Her voice was so powerful that it penetrated the thick freezer walls and could be heard all over the kitchen and dining lodge.

Makes 1 loaf

       5   tablespoons unsalted butter, softened
   1¼   cups Sucanat (dehydrated cane juice)
           or brown sugar
       2   eggs
       1   cup mashed ripe banana
    ⅓   cup buttermilk
       1   cup unbleached all-purpose flour
       1   cup whole wheat pastry flour
    ½   cup unsweetened coconut
    ½   teaspoon baking powder
       1   teaspoon baking soda
    ½   teaspoon sea salt

In a food processor or a mixing bowl, cream the butter and Sucanat or brown sugar until it's a smooth paste. Add the eggs and beat for 2 minutes more; then add the mashed banana and buttermilk, beating for 1 minute more.

Sift the flours, coconut, baking powder, baking soda, and salt into a mixing bowl. Add the wet ingredients to this mixture and gently stir with a wooden spoon until mixed. Pour into a greased and floured bread pan and bake in a preheated oven at 350 degrees F for 1 hour or until a knife inserted into the bread comes out clean. Take out of pan and place on a wire rack to cool.

COMPANY'S COMING SCONES

This is another recipe brought to the Esalen kitchen by Bill Herr. He wrote, "These delicately textured scones are made without butter. (That hardly makes them low-cal, however, since they're made with cream instead!) Thirty scones may sound like a lot, but you can't eat just one, and besides, company's coming."

Makes 30 scones

- 2 cups raisins (or other dried fruit such as currants, dried cranberries, apricots, or figs)*
- 6 cups unbleached all-purpose flour
- 3 tablespoons non-aluminum baking powder
- 1 teaspoon salt
- 1 cup sugar
- 4 cups whipping cream
  Milk for brushing tops
  Coarse sugar for sprinkling (optional)

If the dried fruit you've chosen is larger than raisins, cut to approximately that size.

Mix dry ingredients together in a large bowl and then add the fruit. Add cream and mix just until combined. Divide dough into three equal parts, and then with a rolling pin or by hand, shape each portion into an 8-inch circle. Cut each circle into 10 wedges, like a pie. Brush tops with milk. Sprinkle with coarse sugar if desired.

Place on a lightly oiled baking sheet with about an inch of space between each scone. Bake in a preheated oven at 375 degrees F for 20 minutes or until they are golden brown.

DARK RUSSIAN
RYE BREAD

Reuben sandwiches have been a popular lunch item at Esalen for many years. This Dark Russian Rye is the bread that we serve our Reubens on, and many people have asked for the recipe over the years. This is the basis for making a great Reuben sandwich.

Makes 2 loaves

      3 cups warm water
  4$\frac{1}{2}$ teaspoons dry active baking yeast
  9$\frac{1}{2}$ cups rye flour
  $\frac{1}{2}$ cup molasses
  $\frac{1}{2}$ cup cocoa powder
      3 tablespoons unsalted butter, melted
      5 teaspoons toasted caraway seeds
  1$\frac{1}{2}$ tablespoons sea salt
      7 cups unbleached all-purpose flour

Place the warm water in a mixing bowl and whisk in the yeast until it is completely dissolved. Place in a draft-free place until it "blooms." Blooming has taken place when the mixture forms a thick foam on the surface. Stir in the rye flour, stirring at least 50 strokes, then cover with a kitchen towel and place in a warm, draft-free spot for about 1/2 hour.

Stir in the molasses, cocoa powder, butter, caraway seeds, and sea salt and blend well. Stir in half of the unbleached flour and incorporate it into the dough. Place the remaining half of the unbleached flour on a kneading surface and drop the dough onto the surface. Knead the dough until it is firm, smooth, and elastic. This can be done by pushing the dough away from you with the heel of one hand, and then folding it back over and toward you with the other hand. Turn the dough a quarter turn and repeat the process. This will take about 10 minutes, and most of the flour on the kneading surface will be incorporated into the dough.

Divide dough in half. Place each half into an oiled bread pan, cover with a kitchen towel, and put in a draft-free, warm spot to raise for 1 hour. Bake in a preheated oven at 350 degrees F for about 45 minutes. Remove from oven and place on a wire rack to cool.

TRUSTEE MUFFIN

This muffin was served for many years as a breakfast special. It got its name by being the breakfast special that was served when Esalen's board of trustees would come down to the property for their monthly meeting.

Makes 15 muffins

- $^2/_3$ cup raisins
- $^3/_4$ cup walnuts
- $1^1/_2$ cups unbleached all-purpose flour
- $1^1/_2$ cups rolled oats
- $^3/_4$ cup brown sugar or Sucanat (dehydrated cane juice)
- $^1/_2$ teaspoon non-aluminum baking powder
- 1 teaspoon baking soda
- $^1/_2$ teaspoon sea salt
- 1 teaspoon cinnamon
- 1 cup grated carrots
- 2 eggs
- 1 cup milk
- $^1/_3$ cup safflower oil
- 1 teaspoon vanilla

Soak the raisins for 15 minutes in a bowl with warm water until soft, then drain well. Chop the walnuts into small chunks. Sift the flour, oats, brown sugar, baking powder, baking soda, salt, and cinnamon in a mixing bowl. Add the carrots, raisins, and walnuts and mix well with the dry ingredients.

In another bowl, thoroughly mix the eggs, milk, oil, and vanilla. Add the wet ingredients to the dry ingredients and mix just enough to blend everything well. Don't overmix. Oil and flour a muffin pan; then fill each muffin cup half full. Bake for 12 to 15 minutes in an oven preheated to 350 degrees F. Muffins are done when a knife inserted into a muffin comes out clean. Turn muffins out of pan and place on a cooling rack.

SOURDOUGH RYE BREAD

This hardy loaf is an authentic Old European bread, having a dense, moist texture and a sour rye taste. It's loaded with sunflower seeds and cooked rye berries. Rye berries are made from whole grain rye that has been cooked until soft. This is an excellent bread for those who are intolerant to wheat. This bread will keep easily for a week.

Makes 2 loaves

2	cups rye berries
4¹/₂	cups water, divided
1¹/₂	cups rye flakes
2	cups sunflower seeds
9	cups rye flour
2	tablespoons salt
1¹/₂	cups sourdough starter (see page 23)

Place the rye berries in a saucepan with 4 cups water; bring to a boil, then lower to a simmer. Simmer for 35 minutes, or until the water has evaporated and the berries are soft. Drain off any liquid and set aside to cool.

Combine the rye flakes and sunflower seeds in a mixing bowl. Add the flour, salt, 1/2 cup water, sourdough starter, and soft rye berries. Stir until well blended. Cover the dough with a kitchen towel and leave at room temperature for 12 hours. The dough should get spongy and will raise about another quarter in size. Divide the dough and place into two oiled bread pans. Smooth the top of the dough with a spatula. This is a sticky dough to the touch.

Cover and place in a draft-free, warm spot to raise for another hour. Bake in an oven preheated to 275 degrees F for 2 to 2¹/₂ hours or until the internal temperature of the dough measures 210 degrees F. Remove from pans and let cool on a wire rack.

This bread is best after it has matured, or set for 12 hours after it is baked. It will keep for days. It should be sliced thin when served.

SPELT SOURDOUGH RAISIN BREAD

Spelt is an ancient grain that migrated from the Middle East into Central Europe, where it was widely cultivated until it was replaced by wheat. True spelt has a very low gluten content. The spelt found in the United States is a hybrid cross between true spelt and wheat. This cross was done to increase the yield per acre because the main drawback with true spelt is its low yield per acre. There has been a small but strong resurgence to cultivate true spelt in Europe. True spelt has a small kernel, resembling short-grain brown rice, with a brown honey color. The marrying of the sourness of the bread and the sweetness of the raisins in this recipe makes a tasty contrast that many people love.

Makes one 9-inch loaf

- 1/3 cup sourdough starter (see page 23)
- 2 cups lukewarm water
- 2 cups unbleached bread flour
- 2 1/2 cups spelt flour
- 1 1/2 tablespoons sea salt
- 1 cup raisins
- 1/4 cup chopped walnuts

In a mixing bowl, whisk the starter and water together, and then whisk in the unbleached bread flour. Place in a warm, draft-free spot for about 10 minutes. Then knead the spelt flour and salt into the dough for 8 minutes. Add the raisins and walnuts and knead for a few minutes to incorporate. Cover with a kitchen towel and let sit for 6 to 12 hours in a warm, draft-free spot. The longer you let the bread raise, the more sour the bread will be.

Place the dough on a lightly floured work surface and knead it for 2 minutes. Put the dough into an oiled 9-inch bread pan, cover, and place in a warm, draft-free spot for another 2 to 3 hours. Bake in an oven preheated to 350 degrees F for about 50 minutes. There are two methods to test if the bread is done: One method is to place a thermometer in the bread—doneness is 190 degrees F interior temperature. The other method is to take the bread out of the pan and thump it with your fingers. The bread should have a hollow sound. When the bread is finished baking, remove it from the pan and place on a wire rack to cool.

HONEY WHOLE WHEAT BREAD

If you have visited the bread bar at the Esalen dining lodge, you have probably come across this basic whole wheat bread. It is one of our staples, and every baker will use this recipe or a variation of it.

Makes 2 loaves

2 1/2	cups warm water
1/4	cup honey
1	tablespoon active dry yeast
3	tablespoons vegetable oil
1	cup dry powdered milk
1	tablespoon sea salt
6–8	cups whole wheat flour

Place the warm water in a mixing bowl; it should be barely warm to the touch. Pour in the honey and gently whisk in the yeast until both the honey and yeast have dissolved. Put bowl in a warm, draft-free spot until the yeast "blooms," or forms a thick foam on the surface.

Mix in the oil, powdered milk, and salt. Stir in the flour, a cup at a time, until the dough becomes too stiff to stir, and then work the dough with your hands. Keep mixing in the flour with your hands until the dough starts to hold together in a ball and does not have a sticky feel when you touch it. Place the remaining flour on a kneading surface and drop the dough onto the kneading surface. Let the dough rest for 5 minutes.

Kneading the remaining dry flour into the wet dough is a very relaxing experience. Knead at least 10 minutes, or until the dough is smooth, firm, and elastic. To knead, push the dough away from you with the heel of one hand, and then fold it back over and toward you with the other hand. Turn the dough a quarter turn and repeat the process. This will stretch and develop the gluten. When the dough forms a smooth dough ball and stops taking up the flour, the kneading process is completed. (Another sign the dough is ready is that it springs slowly back into place when you poke it with your finger.)

Return the dough to the mixing bowl, cover with a clean kitchen towel, and place in a warm, draft-free place for about 1 hour or until the dough has doubled in size. Take it out of the bowl and knead for about 2 minutes more. Then divide the dough in half, shape into loaves, and place into 2 oiled bread pans. Cover and return pans to the raising place and let raise for about 40 minutes or until the dough has doubled.

Bake in a preheated oven at 350 degrees F for 40 minutes to 1 hour. There are two methods to determine when the bread is done: You can place a thermometer into a loaf; it should read between 190 to 200 degrees F. Or you can take a loaf out of the oven and tap it with your fingers on the bottom. It should have a hollow sound. When bread is done baking, remove it from the oven and cool on a wire rack.

Semolina Sourdough Bread

SEMOLINA SOURDOUGH BREAD

This is a true sourdough bread, but because of the semolina flour it doesn't have a dense texture like most sourdough breads. The pumpkin and sunflower seeds give it a nice crunch.

Makes one 9-inch loaf

- 2 cups lukewarm water
- 1/3 cup sourdough starter (see page 23)
- 1 1/4 cups unbleached bread flour
- 3 cups semolina flour
- 1 teaspoon salt
- 1/4 cup pumpkin seeds
- 1/4 cup sunflower seeds

In a large bowl, whisk the water and sourdough starter together, and then whisk in the bread flour and let it sit in a warm, draft-free spot for 10 minutes. Stir in the semolina flour and the salt and knead for 8 minutes.

Knead the seeds into the bread and cover with a kitchen towel. Let the dough sit in a warm, draft-free spot for 6 to 12 hours. The longer the bread is left to raise, the more sour the taste will be.

Lightly flour a work surface and knead the dough on it for 2 minutes; then place the bread into an oiled 9-inch bread pan and leave to raise for another 2 to 3 hours. The dough should raise another 70 percent of its original size. Bake in a preheated oven at 350 degrees F for approximately 50 minutes. There are two methods for testing if the bread is done: You can place a thermometer into the bread—doneness is 190 degrees F. Or you can take the bread out of the pan and tap the bottom with your fingers. It should sound hollow. When bread is finished baking, remove it from the pan and let cool on a wire rack.

BREAKFASTS

Buttermilk Biscuits | 46

Sponges of Love Pancakes | 48

Sweet & Spicy Breakfast Polenta | 49

Apple & Almond Rice Cereal | 49

Maple-Walnut Breakfast Cake | 51

Polenta Pancakes | 52

Marion's Living Muesli | 55

Esalen Granola | 56

Bagels | 58

BISCUIT-MAKING TECHNIQUES

After making several thousand biscuits, I've concluded good biscuits are more a result of technique rather than recipe. In a nutshell, the technique is to minimize the handling of the ingredients at all stages. The key steps are as follows:

1. Butter handling: Grating frozen butter is a simple and efficient way to get it to almost the right size for biscuit making. The process of integrating butter into the flour mixture by hand then quickly completes the job and the butter remains chilled.

2. Liquid incorporation: Combining the wet and dry ingredients is less about "kneading" than just forming the dough into a coherent mass.

3. Biscuit cutting: Using a sharp-edged cutter leads to higher and more even raising of biscuits. Also, cut straight down; twisting the cutter can lead to uneven raising.

BUTTERMILK BISCUITS

Bill Herr has done many jobs in the Esalen kitchen, from dishwasher to manager. He is an excellent baker and will always be known as Esalen's best biscuit maker. Here, in his own words, is some of Bill's biscuit talk: "Being raised in Texas, I got my share of biscuits and gravy as a kid. This made me aware of the amazing variety of what passes for a biscuit. When I first made biscuits in the Esalen kitchen, I got the first of several lessons in the difference between making a dozen and making 20 dozen. The one constant though is remembering to handle the dough gently."

Makes 16 biscuits

- 3 cups unbleached all-purpose flour
- 2 tablespoons non-aluminum baking powder
- 1/2 teaspoon baking soda
- 1 teaspoon salt
- 6 tablespoons unsalted butter, frozen
- 1 cup buttermilk
  Melted butter for brushing tops (optional)
  Buttermilk for brushing tops (optional)

Combine the first four dry ingredients and mix well.

Grate frozen butter through large holes in grater. Very briefly, work butter into flour mixture by hand until the butter pieces are pea-sized. Make a well in the center of the dry ingredients and add the buttermilk. Combine just until the ingredients are moistened.

Turn out onto lightly floured board and form dough into a disk about 12 inches in diameter, kneading the dough only 3 or 4 times to bring it together. Cut the biscuits by pressing the cutter straight down. Don't twist the cutter through the dough. Cut the biscuits so as to minimize the excess dough or "scrap." For crispy-sided biscuits, place them 1 to 2 inches apart on an ungreased baking sheet. For soft-sided biscuits, place them only about 1/2 inch apart.

For a golden glaze, brush biscuits with melted butter. For a more brown crust, brush them with buttermilk. Bake for 12 to 15 minutes in an oven preheated to 425 degrees F.

FRUIT GLAZE

For a simple sweet glaze, top each biscuit with a sugar cube briefly soaked in fruit juice concentrate.

SPONGES OF LOVE PANCAKES

John Blunt has been working in the Esalen kitchen for the last 12 years, holding staff chef and manager positions during that time. Sponges of Love Pancakes is by far one of the best remembered breakfast recipes coming out of the Esalen kitchen. When asked about this recipe, here is what John said: "I was encouraged by the staff to serve pancakes for breakfast. I wanted to create a light, fluffy pancake and so I started to experiment on my Monday morning breakfast shift. It took me about 15 tries before I had the current recipe down. I wanted to call the pancakes Moon Cakes, because I served them on the day of the moon, Monday. But the staff gave them the name that has stuck today: Sponges of Love. The name came about because people loved how the pancakes soaked up the butter and maple syrup like a sponge. One of the staff members calculated that I've served approximately 300,000 pancakes since I started flipping them on the Esalen griddle."

Makes 8 to 10 (6-inch) pancakes

- 4 cups unbleached all-purpose flour
- 3/4 teaspoon sea salt
- 4 tablespoons non-aluminum baking powder
- 4 eggs
- 3/4 cup vegetable oil
- 3 cups buttermilk
- 1 cup water

Sift the flour, salt, and baking powder into a 3-quart mixing bowl. In another mixing bowl, whisk the oil and eggs until well blended; then stir in buttermilk and water. Stir as you pour the wet ingredients into the dry ingredients. Mix only until the batter is blended. Don't overmix.

The batter will be thick, almost looking like a sponge. Cook in a heavy-bottomed frying pan or a cast-iron skillet. Heat the pan over medium-high heat, and then put a drop of vegetable oil into the pan and spread it around with a paper towel until the bottom of the pan is covered with a fine film of oil.

Use a ladle for scooping out the batter; gently shake the ladle so the batter will drop onto the skillet. When bubbles start to appear around the edges of the pancakes and the centers appear dry, flip them with a spatula and cook on the other side. Gently flip the pancakes so they don't lose their spongy loft. With the right pan temperature, cooking time should be about $2\frac{1}{2}$ minutes for each side.

SWEET & SPICY
BREAKFAST POLENTA

This is a sweet and spicy breakfast cereal that has a hearty, warming effect on the body. The cardamom, cinnamon, and fresh ginger give this recipe an Indian infusion, and the sweetness of the honey complements and balances the fiery taste of the ginger. What a way to start the day!

Makes 4 servings

    4   cups milk
  1/4   cup honey
  1/2   teaspoon salt
1 1/2   teaspoons ground cardamom
    1   teaspoon cinnamon
    1   tablespoon grated fresh ginger
  3/4   cup polenta

In a 2-quart saucepan over medium-high heat, bring the milk, honey, salt, cardamom, cinnamon, and ginger to a boil, constantly stirring to avoid burning the milk. Slowly pour in the polenta as you whisk the liquid briskly. Lower the heat to simmer and cook 10 to 15 minutes, stirring frequently. Serve hot.

APPLE & ALMOND
RICE CEREAL

This is the most common way that we use up leftover rice from the last night's dinners at Esalen. It has turned into a staple item on the Esalen breakfast bar. This cereal has no dairy and no wheat so it will fit almost everyone's diet. The rice milk gives this healthy breakfast a unique taste, although you could use any type of milk you choose with this recipe.

Makes 4 servings

    2   cups cooked rice
  1/2   cup raisins
    2   cups rice milk
  1/2   cup chopped, toasted almonds (walnuts, hazelnuts, or cashews may be substituted)
    1   medium-size apple (about 1 1/2 cups), finely chopped (pears, peaches, or fresh berries may be substituted)
    1   teaspoon vanilla

This cereal is best if you can soak the rice and raisins in the rice milk the night before, but you can also prepare it just before serving. Place the rice into a 1-quart saucepan. Add the rice milk and raisins and place over high heat. Bring to a boil. When the mixture starts to boil, lower the heat to simmer and add the almonds, apple, and vanilla. Let simmer until the rice milk is reduced and the mixture has a thick consistency like oatmeal. Remove from the heat and cover for 5 to 10 minutes to allow the cereal to set up. Serve warm.

Maple-Walnut Breakfast Cake

MAPLE-WALNUT
BREAKFAST CAKE

This is one of the best vegan breakfast cakes I've tasted. People eating it never would know that its rich taste had no animal ingredients. Katie Armstrong developed this recipe when she was a staff cook. Katie was one of those young pioneers who came to Big Sur in the early '70s to live off the grid in a self-sufficient lifestyle. She had cooking experience around some of the resorts in Big Sur, and when she asked me for a job, all I had open at the time was a night dishwasher. She took it, washing dishes and mopping floors for six months until an opening came available working behind the stoves.

Makes 9 slices

- 1 3/4   cups unbleached all-purpose flour
- 1 1/2   cups Sucanat (dehydrated cane juice)
          or sugar
- 1 1/2   teaspoons baking soda
-   1/2   teaspoon salt
-     2   teaspoons cinnamon
-     1   teaspoon ground ginger
- 1 1/2   cups water
-   1/2   cup oil
-   1/4   cup maple syrup
-   1/4   cup apple cider vinegar
-     1   teaspoon vanilla
-   1/2   cup chopped walnuts

In a mixing bowl, sift all the dry ingredients together.

In another mixing bowl, whisk into the water, one at a time, all the wet ingredients. Add the wet ingredients to the dry and beat just until smoothly blended. Pour into an oiled 9- x 11-inch baking pan and sprinkle the chopped walnuts over the top. Bake in a preheated oven at 350 degrees F for approximately 40 minutes, or until a knife inserted into the cake comes out clean. Place on a wire rack and cool.

POLENTA PANCAKES

When I was the breakfast chef at Esalen, I'd come into the kitchen around 7:00 a.m. I would put Chopin on the music system, and then light the ovens. The Chopin set the early morning mood for the work scholars who would be filing in for the morning shift. I remember telling them that the Esalen ovens would not light unless Chopin was played to them!

Makes about 12 pancakes

- 1/2 cup unbleached all-purpose flour
- 1 tablespoon baking powder
- 1/2 teaspoon salt
- 1 cup cornmeal
- 1/2 cup polenta
- 2 tablespoons Sucanat (dehydrated cane juice) or brown sugar
- 1 egg
- 2 cups milk
- 2 teaspoons oil
- 1 teaspoon lemon juice
- 1/2 teaspoon vanilla

Sift into a mixing bowl the flour, baking powder, and salt. Add the cornmeal, polenta, and the Sucanat or brown sugar and blend well.

In two bowls, separate the white from the yoke of the egg. In a small bowl, pour in the 2 cups of milk; add the oil and whisk until blended. Then beat in the egg yoke, lemon juice, and vanilla. Stir this mixture into the dry ingredients until it is just combined.

With a hand blender or whisk, beat the egg white until it has stiff peaks, and then gently fold it into the pancake batter. Heat an oiled skillet over medium-high heat, then pour 1/4 cup of the batter into the skillet and let cook until small bubbles appear over the surface of the pancake. Flip the pancake over and cook the other side until browned. Don't flip the pancake again or it will lose its fluffy lightness. Beating the egg whites separately makes these pancakes light and lofty, and the polenta gives them a slight crunch.

MARION'S LIVING MUESLI

This recipe was taken from the Esalen Cleanse. The Cleanse is an annual Raw and Live Food workshop that is offered only to the Esalen staff. Each morning breakfast would be a different variation of this tasty, healthy recipe. There was so much demand for it that it was incorporated as one of the weekly breakfast specials on the regular menu.

Makes 2 servings

- 3 tablespoons whole oat groats
- 1 ounce hazelnuts (about 15 nuts)
- 1 tablespoon hulled sunflower seeds
- 1 banana
- 1 apple
- 1 tablespoon flax seed oil (optional)
- 1 tablespoon maple syrup
- 1 teaspoon lemon juice
- 1 tablespoon bee pollen (optional)

In a bowl, soak the oats, hazelnuts, and sunflower seeds overnight in 3 times the amount of water. Soaking the oats, nuts, and seeds in water overnight washes out the enzyme inhibitors and gives birth to the sprouting process. Sprouting transforms the stored energy in nuts, seeds, and grains (the fats and carbs) into active energy to grow a tree or plant (protein and simple sugars).

Place the oats, nuts, and seeds in a colander the next morning and rinse well. Discard the soaking water. Chop the hazelnuts in half. Place all of the mixture in a mixing bowl. Chop the banana into bite-size rounds and grate the apple; add both to the mixing bowl.

Place the oil (if using), syrup, lemon juice, and pollen (if using) together in a cup and beat with a fork until blended. Pour this liquid over the muesli mixture and gently toss all ingredients until mixed.

ESALEN GRANOLA

Housemade granola is an old favorite at Esalen, going back to almost the beginning of the institute. The recipe has changed over the years, but this favorite breakfast cereal has never lost its dedicated appeal. Making your own granola is far superior in quality and nutrition to the supermarket variety, which is usually loaded with refined sugars and cheap oils. Feel free to substitute different flakes, sweeteners, nuts, seeds, and flavorings to create your own recipe.

Makes about 3 pounds

8	cups rolled oats
1	cup rye flakes
1	cup whole almonds, coarsely chopped
1	cup whole cashews, coarsely chopped
1/2	cup sunflower seeds
2	teaspoons cinnamon
1	teaspoon sea salt
3/4	cup honey
3/4	cup maple syrup
1/2	cup vegetable oil
2	tablespoons vanilla

In a mixing bowl, blend the oats, rye, almonds, cashews, sunflower seeds, cinnamon, and salt.

In a small saucepan, mix the honey, syrup, oil, and vanilla. Stir over low heat until this is well blended; then pour the liquid into the dry ingredients and mix until everything is blended.

Spread a 1/2-inch-thick layer of the wet granola on two 12- x 16-inch baking sheets. Bake in a preheated oven at 325 degrees F for 1 hour, or until the granola turns golden brown. Be sure to turn every 5 to 10 minutes. Remove baking sheets from oven and allow granola to cool.

BAGELS

This recipe was one of those Sunday brunch meals that created a lot of excitement in the Esalen kitchen as well as in the dining lodge. This recipe was perfected by Liam McDermott in the Esalen bakery. The bagels were made fresh from scratch. Kitchen staff who had never before experienced the chance to make fresh bagels were elated with their accomplishment, and seminarians who had never had a fresh bagel "homemade style" were equally excited to discover something new.

Makes 14 bagels

1	tablespoon dry active baking yeast
	Pinch sugar
2½	cups lukewarm water (90 to 100 degrees F)
7¼	cups unbleached all-purpose flour
1	cup whole wheat flour
2	eggs
1	tablespoon salt
2	tablespoons vegetable oil
2	tablespoons molasses
3	quarts water
½	cup molasses

In a mixing bowl, stir the yeast and sugar into the water until dissolved. Place in a warm spot until the mixture "blooms" (a foam will appear on the surface). Then add 3½ cups unbleached flour and 1 cup whole wheat flour, stirring until the flour is dissolved into the mixture. Let stand for about 30 to 45 minutes in a warm spot to raise. You will know it's ready when air bubbles start to escape from the mixture and it looks like a sponge.

In a separate bowl, beat together the eggs, salt, oil, and 2 tablespoons molasses. Stir this into the flour mixture until smooth.

Add 3¾ cups of unbleached flour into the mixture, stirring at first, and then kneading the mixture into a firm dough. Roll into a ball, and place in a large oiled mixing bowl, turning the dough to oil all sides. Cover with a kitchen towel. Place in a warm, draft-free spot to rise for about 1½ hours. Rising time will depend on how warm or drafty the room, how active the yeast, and how warm the ingredients. The dough should double in size.

Separate dough into 14 individual 1/4-pound pieces, about the size of tennis balls. Knead the air out of each piece until you have a tight dough ball, then let it rest for 10 minutes to relax the dough. With your thumbs, poke a hole into the dough ball and gently stretch it out to form a doughnut shape. Let the bagel rest for 3 to 4 minutes.

In the widest saucepan you have, add 3 quarts of water and 1/2 cup of molasses. Bring to a boil, and then lower to a gentle simmer. Drop the bagel into the water for 20 seconds and then, with a slotted spoon, turn the bagel and cook on the other side for 20 seconds. Be sure not to leave the bagel in the simmering water for more than 2 minutes or you will kill the yeast. Place bagels on a baking sheet that has been oiled or lined with parchment paper and bake for 20 minutes at 350 degrees F. Cool on a wire rack.

BAGEL TOPPINGS

Different toppings can be added to the outside of the bagels before they are put into the oven. You can be creative with toppings, adding or blending many different ingredients. At Esalen we top our bagels with minced onion, minced garlic, poppy seeds, sesame seeds, and sunflower seeds.

LUNCHES

Artichoke, Yam, & Blue Cheese Scones | 62

Chard Cakes (aka Esalen Garden Cakes) | 63

Egg Foo Yong | 65

Green Chile Macaroni & Cheese | 66

Leek & Onion Tart | 69

Griddle Corn Cakes | 71

Yam & Black Bean Burrito | 72

Provençal Veggie Turnovers | 75

Greek Quiche | 77

ARTICHOKE, YAM, & BLUE CHEESE SCONES

These savory scones are a meal in themselves. They are an interesting blend of quartered artichokes, sweet yams, and creamy pungent blue cheese. The addition of the aromatic flavor of sage brings the mouth alive with a multitude of tastes! These scones also make a delightful lunch served with a salad or soup.

Makes 8 scones

- 1 large yellow onion
- 1 tablespoon vegetable oil
- 2 medium-size yams
- 8 ounces (small can) artichoke hearts in water
- 1 3/4 cups unbleached all-purpose flour
- 1 1/2 cups whole wheat flour
- 1/2 teaspoon baking soda
- 1 1/2 teaspoons non-aluminum baking powder
- 1 teaspoon sea salt
  Pinch cayenne pepper
- 1 cup unsalted butter
- 2 1/2 cups grated Asiago cheese
- 1/2 pound crumbled blue cheese
- 2 tablespoons chopped fresh sage

Chop the onion into 1/2-inch dice and sauté in a skillet with a small amount of oil until brown. Peel and chop the yams into 1/2-inch cubes, and then lightly steam until cooked but still firm. Drain the artichoke hearts and cut in quarters. Put the onion, yams, and artichoke hearts in a large bowl and set aside.

Sift flours, baking soda, baking powder, salt, and cayenne pepper in mixing bowl. Cut butter into 1-inch chunks. Add butter to the dry ingredients and cut in with a pastry cutter until the mixture is the size of peas. Gently fold in the Asiago cheese and half of the blue cheese.

Mix the sage into the yam mixture and fold the mixture into the dough; briefly mix until the dough comes together. Don't over-mix. This dough should have a chunky appearance and a sticky texture. If the dough is not sticky, add a small amount of liquid (buttermilk, milk, or water) to create a sticky texture.

Using an ice cream scoop or a large spoon, scoop out baseball-size balls of dough and place on a greased baking sheet. Flatten the ball with a fork, making a small depression on top. Place the remaining blue cheese in the depressions on top the scones. Bake in a preheated oven at 350 degrees F for approximately 30 minutes or until the scone is light brown. Place on a wire rack to cool.

CHARD CAKES (AKA ESALEN GARDEN CAKES)

At Esalen, we count the days of the month by "Changeover Monday." Every twenty-eight days in the Esalen kitchen, we receive fourteen new work scholars. Kitchen work scholars are people who come for a four-week workshop, and they receive a reduced fee for working thirty-two hours a week doing kitchen chores. Changeover Monday is the first day of the new work scholar kitchen crew, and this is the only training day the new recruits have. Chard Cakes were always on the menu because that was a meal that one cook could prepare alone, leaving the work scholars to train for their new job. The long-time staff would recognize "Changeover Monday" by this classic nutritious lunch. It's a tasty way to get your daily dose of green vegetables.

Makes 4 to 6 cakes

CHARD CAKES

- 4 eggs
- 1/2 teaspoon sea salt
- 2 tablespoons water
- 1/2 medium-sized onion
- 1/2 pound swiss chard, washed and patted dry with paper towel
- 1 tablespoon sesame oil for frying

DILL & HORSERADISH GOAT CHEESE SAUCE

- 1/2 pound soft goat cheese or sour cream
- 1 tablespoon milk or water
- 1 tablespoon prepared horseradish
- 1 tablespoon fresh dill
- 1/4 teaspoon sea salt

To make the Chard Cakes, crack eggs into a mixing bowl, add salt and water, and beat with a whisk or fork until light and fluffy. Slice the onion into small half-moon slices. Cut stems from the leaves of the chard and chop the stems into fine strips. Lay the chard leaves one on top of another, roll up into a tight cigar-like shape, and slice into fine ribbons. Add the chard and onion to the egg mixture and mix well.

Heat the oil in a frying pan and, with a large spoon, scoop up the egg and veggie mixture and drop into the pan. Cook until golden brown, approximately 4 minutes; turn with a spatula and brown the other side. Serve with Dill & Horseradish Goat Cheese Sauce on top.

To make the Dill & Horseradish Goat Cheese Sauce, mash the goat cheese in a mixing bowl with the milk or water and horseradish until you have a smooth sauce-like consistency. Then add the dill. Serve over Chard Cakes.

Egg Foo Yong

EGG FOO YONG

These small Chinese omelets are packed with flavor and are easy to prepare. The shiitake mushrooms have a meaty flavor and savory texture that blends well with the crunchy vegetables and slight perk of the fresh ginger.

Makes 8 servings

- 1 cup mung bean sprouts
- 1 cup grated carrots
- 1 cup thinly sliced shiitake mushrooms
- 1 cup $1/2$-inch slices snow peas
- 1 teaspoon minced garlic
- $1/2$ cup finely sliced green onions
- 2 cups shredded Napa cabbages (Chinese cabbage) or bok choy
- 1 cup $1/2$-inch dice red bell pepper
- 3 tablespoons cilantro
- 2 teaspoons grated ginger
- 6 eggs
- $1 3/4$ teaspoons sea salt
- Pinch cayenne pepper
- 2 tablespoons vegetable oil

Mix all the vegetables and the cilantro and ginger together in a mixing bowl. In a separate bowl, whisk the eggs with the salt and cayenne pepper. Pour the egg mixture into the vegetables and toss until the vegetables are completely coated with the egg.

Heat the oil in a skillet over medium-high heat, and then drop one large spoonful of the vegetable mixture (draining off the excess egg) into the pan. Press the vegetables down to a 1/2-inch thickness with a fork. Cook until brown on one side, about 3 minutes, and then flip and brown the other side. Serve with tamari gravy.

TAMARI GRAVY

- 1 green onion, chopped in fine rounds
- 1 teaspoon minced garlic
- 1 tablespoon vegetable oil
- $1/2$ cup tamari natural soy sauce
- 4 cups vegetable stock or water
- $1/4$ cup arrowroot or cornstarch
- 2 tablespoons chopped parsley

In a 2-quart saucepan on high heat, sauté the onions and garlic in the oil for 2 minutes. Add tamari and sauté for 1 minute more. Add liquid, bring to a boil, lower heat to simmer and cover. Let simmer for 1/2 hour.

Mix arrowroot with a small amount of cold water to make a paste the consistency of sour cream. Add this to the sauce, raise heat to high, and stir until thick. Add chopped parsley and serve over Egg Foo Yong.

GREEN CHILE
MACARONI & CHEESE

Macaroni and cheese is a classic example of an American comfort meal. Using this comfort food as a base, Esalen created many tasty variations of it, including this one that is a favorite at the Esalen lodge.

Makes 6 servings

5	quarts water
1 1/2	tablespoons salt (for cooking the macaroni)
1	pound elbow macaroni
5	tablespoons unsalted butter
6	tablespoons unbleached all-purpose flour
2	teaspoons salt
1	teaspoon pasilla chile powder
1	can (8 ounces) mild green chile strips, drained and finely diced
1	jalapeno pepper, seeded and finely chopped
5	cups milk
2	cups grated pepper jack cheese
2	cups grated sharp cheddar cheese
4	scallions, chopped in small rounds
1	bag Mexican-flavored corn chips (or regular corn chips)

Pulse corn chips in a food processor approximately 10 times until they are small to medium crumbs. If you don't have a food processor, place them in a plastic bag and crush with a rolling pin. Set aside for topping.

In a large pot, bring 5 quarts of water to boil. Add the 1 1/2 tablespoons salt and the macaroni, stirring as you pour the pasta into the water. Cook the pasta, stirring occasionally, until it is chewy but firm (al dente). Drain the pasta and rinse in cold water; then set aside.

In a heavy-bottomed saucepan, melt the butter over medium heat until it starts to bubble, and then whisk in the flour, 2 teaspoons salt, and chile powder. Whisk until it forms a paste; then add the green chile strips and the jalapeno pepper, stirring constantly. Add the milk and stir until the mixture boils; then reduce the heat to low and cook slowly until sauce is thick. Cut off the heat and slowly sprinkle in the cheese, whisking or stirring until the cheese is fully melted. Add the cooked pasta, turn the heat to low, and simmer for about 5 minutes. Pour into a 9- x 11-inch baking dish and cover with crumbled corn-chip topping. Bake at 350 degrees F for about 20 minutes.

*Green Chile
Macaroni & Cheese*

Leek & Onion Tart

LEEK & ONION TART

This is a classic dish of Nice, France. You will find it on menus in restaurants there as well as in the many bakeries in the Old Quarter. We serve it as a lunch dish at Esalen. Except for the addition of the whole wheat flour, it was in this original form when I started to prepare it at Esalen. As I was pulled away from the cooking line and spent more time in the kitchen office, many other cooks explored this recipe and created their own variations of this yummy lunch.

Makes 6 to 8 servings

CRUST

1	teaspoon brown sugar
1 1/4	cups lukewarm water (about 110 degrees F)
1 1/2	teaspoons dry active baking yeast
3 1/4	cups unbleached bread flour
1/4	cup vegetable oil
1	teaspoon salt
1	cup whole wheat bread flour

FILLING

2	pounds yellow onions
4	medium-size leeks
1	teaspoon olive oil
1	tablespoon fresh thyme
1/2	teaspoon salt
1 1/4	cups grated Asiago or Parmesan cheese
1/2	cup chopped oil-cured olives
1	small tin anchovies, drained

The crust for this tart is similar to thin-crust pizza dough, having to raise only once. To make the crust, in a nonmetal mixing bowl, dissolve the sugar into the water and then slowly whisk the yeast into the liquid and set aside for the mixture to "bloom." The bloom usually takes 5 to 10 minutes—bubbles will rise and a frothy head will develop on top.

Using a wooden spoon, slowly stir 1 1/4 cups unbleached flour into the mixture until it is smooth. Then stir the dough rapidly for about 5 minutes, cover, and let rest for 5 minutes. This helps to develop the gluten.

Stir the oil and salt into the dough until thoroughly mixed. Slowly stir in the whole wheat flour until smooth. When finished, stir in the remaining unbleached flour. You may find it easier to use your hands to mix in the last part of the unbleached flour, adding a little and then kneading it into the dough, then adding a little more flour, and so on until you have a firm, nonsticky dough.

Knead the dough for another 5 minutes. You can do this by pushing the dough away from you with the heel of one hand, then folding it back over and toward you with the other hand. Turn the dough one-fourth turn and repeat the procedure. When finished kneading, return dough to the bowl and cover it with a kitchen towel. Place in a warm, draft-free spot to raise until the dough doubles in size (about 45 minutes).

Continued on next page

When the dough has doubled, place it on a floured board and roll it out to the shape of your pizza pan, cookie sheet, or baking pan. Rotate the dough as you roll, and flip it over, until you roll it out to the size of the pan. The dough should hang over the edge all the way around. Place the dough gently into the pan and roll up the edge to form a rim that will hold the onion mixture.

While the dough is raising, prepare the filling. Peel and chop the onions in thin, half-moon slices. Slit the leeks down the side, and then rinse under running water to remove any dirt. Chop into 1/4-inch rounds. Heat olive oil in a sauté pan over high heat and sauté the onions and leeks until the onions turn translucent. Lower the heat to medium and sauté until the onions turn a golden brown. Add the thyme and salt; mix well.

After placing the dough into the pan, place one-third of the cheese on the dough to lightly cover the bottom. Then evenly spread the onion mixture over the dough. Sprinkle the remaining cheese over the onion mixture. Place chopped olives over the cheese and anchovy fillets over the olives. Bake in a preheated oven at 400 degrees F for about 45 minutes or until you can see the edges of the crust turn light brown. The tart, like pizza, is best served warm.

GRIDDLE CORN CAKES

Corn and potatoes were staples for many of the Indian nations of the Americas. Although we have no way to verify it, this savory little cake could have been a recipe of those early inhabitants. At one time it was a favorite lunch item in our dining lodge. It tastes best served with a Chipotle Cream Sauce (see recipe on page 174).

Makes 8 cakes

- 3/4 pound Yukon Gold potatoes
- 2 large ears fresh corn or 2 1/2 cups frozen corn
- 1 teaspoon ground cumin
- 4 tablespoons bread crumbs
- 2 teaspoons chile powder
- 2 teaspoons fresh chopped cilantro
- 1 teaspoon sea salt
- 1 egg
  Oil for frying

If you can't find Yukon Gold potatoes, use a creamy rather than a mealy type of potato for this recipe, such as Yellow Finn, white, or red potatoes. Do not use Russet or baking potatoes.

Wash the potatoes and leave the peel on. Grate potatoes with a food processor or a hand grater. Cut the kernels from the ears of corn and scrape the pulp from the cut ears with a fork. The pulp will help hold the corn cake together. If using frozen corn, puree 1/2 cup of corn in a blender. Place this with the corn kernels into a mixing bowl with the grated potatoes.

Toast the cumin in a dry frying pan over medium heat. Toss cumin into the corn-and-potato mixture and add the bread crumbs, chile powder, cilantro, and salt, blending everything thoroughly.

In a separate bowl, beat the egg. Stir it into the mixture. Heat a small amount of oil in a frying pan over medium heat and drop a scoop of the mixture into the pan. Flatten the mixture with a fork in one hand and a spoon in the other; hold the spoon on the edge of the cake and press with the fork to form an escalope, or cutlet, shape. The corn cakes should be about 3/8 inch thick. Fry on one side until brown, about 4 minutes, and flip over to brown the other side. Serve with a fresh salsa and Chipotle Cream Sauce.

YAM & BLACK BEAN BURRITO

Anthony Giacobbe, Rachel Fann, and Matt Glazer

Angela Karegeannes brought this recipe to Esalen. When I ask her how she created this recipe, this was her answer: "I came up with the seasoning ideas for this burrito during my college years when I used to go to see Phish, a now-retired rock band. One night at Deer Creek Amphitheater I decided that adding cinnamon to the beans might warm the bellies of my burrito-buying friends, and I also had some limes on hand to add to the burrito. I'll never forget people coming up to me and smiling, saying, 'Wow! What's that smell?' Adding the yams to the mix came later at Esalen when I learned how perfectly cinnamon complements winter vegetables of all kinds."

Makes 6 servings

$3/4$ cup dry black beans
      or about 2 cups canned cooked black beans

2   cloves garlic

1   teaspoon sea salt

2   tablespoons vegetable oil, divided

$1/2$ medium yellow onion, cut into $1/2$-inch dice
      Juice of 1 lime

1   teaspoon cocoa powder
      Pinch brown sugar

2   teaspoons cumin

4   medium Roma tomatoes, cut into $1/2$-inch dice

2   medium ears of fresh corn or 2 cups frozen corn

$1/2$ teaspoon cinnamon

1   large yam, cut into $1/2$-inch dice

2   Anaheim chiles, roasted, peeled, and cut into $1/2$-inch dice

1   teaspoon oregano

2   cups grated sharp cheddar cheese

6   burrito-size flour tortillas (10-inch diameter)

$1/4$ teaspoon cayenne pepper

To cook the beans, use the quick soak method. Put beans into a pot with 4 times the amount of water. Bring to a boil over high heat and then turn off the heat, cover the beans, and let sit for 1 hour. Drain in a colander and rinse well with water. Place the beans back into the pot, adding 4 times the amount of water, along with the whole cloves of garlic and the salt. Bring to a boil and then reduce the heat to simmer. Cook until tender, about 1 hour, and then drain and let cool.

Heat 1 tablespoon of oil in a skillet over high heat, and then sauté the onion for 2 minutes or until the onion becomes translucent. Reduce the heat to low and cook until the onions are brown and caramelized. Blend in the juice of 1 lime, cocoa powder, brown sugar, cayenne, and cumin, and then stir in the tomatoes, corn, and cinnamon. Cook for 5 minutes.

In a separate pan, heat the remaining 1 tablespoon of oil on high. Add the diced yams and sauté until al dente. Then lower the heat and add the chiles and oregano. Continue to sauté until the yams are fork-tender.

On a flat work surface, lay out a tortilla and estimate how much one-sixth of each ingredient will be. On the lower third of the tortilla, place a layer of cheese, followed by a layer of beans. Then do the same with the onion mixture and the yams. Fold and tuck the outer edges of the tortilla inward, and then tightly roll the burrito away from you, tucking in the ends as you roll. Place the burritos on an oiled baking pan and bake in a preheated oven at 350 degrees F until bubbly, about 25 minutes.

Provencal Veggie Turnovers

PROVENÇAL VEGGIE TURNOVERS

The fresh Provencal herbs in this turnover filling are really what make this dish a great success. If these herbs are unavailable fresh, you can substitute dry herbs, but reduce the measure given by half.

Makes 8 turnovers

- ¼ cup unsoaked sun-dried tomatoes
- 1 medium red onion
- 1 red bell pepper
- 1 green bell pepper
- 1 medium-size zucchini
- 2 tablespoons olive oil
- 2 tablespoons chopped fresh basil
- 2 teaspoons chopped fresh thyme
- 2 teaspoons chopped fresh rosemary
- 2 teaspoons chopped fresh oregano
- 2 teaspoons chopped fresh sage
- 2½ cups grated Parmesan cheese
- 1 box of puff pastry, cut into 8 equal squares

Soak the sun-dried tomatoes in a bowl with warm water until tender, about 15 minutes, then drain, chop into julienne strips, and set aside. Chop remaining vegetables into 1-inch cubes. In a sauté pan, heat olive oil over medium heat, and then add onion and sauté for 2 minutes. Add bell peppers and zucchini and sauté until tender. Add sun-dried tomato strips and cook for 1 minute more. Put the mixture into a colander and drain.

Place this mixture in a mixing bowl, add the cheese and herbs, and stir until well blended.

Lay the pastry squares in a diamond shape in front of you. Place a large spoonful of filling in the lower part of each diamond, leaving a 1/2-inch pastry border around the edge. Brush this edge lightly with water using your finger or a brush. Fold over the other half of the diamond and press edges together with a fork. You now have triangular filled turnovers. Place filled turnovers on a baking sheet that has been oiled or lined with parchment paper and bake in a preheated oven at 350 degrees F for 25 minutes or until turnovers are golden brown. Remove from oven and set on a wire rack until cool. If you have any leftover filling, this mixture goes well over rice or pasta.

Greek Quiche

GREEK QUICHE

This is a quiche that's really attractive, with cherry tomatoes, feta cheese, and eggs baked on top. Loaded with fresh herbs and spinach, it makes a great lunch with a side salad.

Makes 6 to 8 servings

CRUST

1³/₄ cups unbleached all-purpose flour

Pinch salt

2 teaspoons dry oregano

¹/₂ cup unsalted butter, chopped into small pieces

6 tablespoons cold water

Olive oil for brushing

FILLING

1 tablespoon extra-virgin olive oil

1 medium red onion, sliced in thin half-moons

2 cloves garlic, minced

1 red bell pepper, chopped in ¹/₄-inch dice

¹/₄ pound button or crimini mushrooms, cut in quarters

1 cup whole cherry tomatoes

³/₄ cup pitted kalamata olives, halved

¹/₄ pound feta cheese, chopped in ¹/₂-inch cubes

2 cups fresh chopped spinach

5 eggs

1 teaspoon chopped fresh sage

1 tablespoon chopped fresh oregano

1 tablespoon chopped fresh parsley

¹/₄ teaspoon sea salt

¹/₂ cup milk

2 tablespoons water

Continued on page 78

To make crust, sift flour and salt into a mixing bowl; add the oregano and butter. Rub the flour and butter together until a fine crumbly texture is formed. Add the cold water and knead gently to form a smooth dough. Let the energy flow from your heart, through your fingertips, and into the pastry. Place the dough in the fridge for 15 to 20 minutes to firm it up.

It's best to use a loose-bottom pie pan with 1½-inch sides when making this quiche, but any 9-inch pie pan will work. On a floured board, roll out the pastry in a circular form. Be careful to not bear down on the rolling pin with too much muscle or you will compact the dough. Slip the pastry over pie pan and gently ease it into place. Roll the edge of the pastry to make a rim. An attractive rim can be made by lifting the pastry over your finger to form pleats. Brush the pastry with a little olive oil to help prevent sogginess. Prick the bottom and sides with a fork and blind bake. Blind baking is done by covering the pastry with parchment paper and then filling the pie shell with dry beans or metal "baking beans" that you find in cooking shops. Bake for 10 minutes at 400 degrees F until the crust starts to turn brown. Take the crust out of the oven and remove the beans and parchment paper. Set aside.

To make the filling, heat the oil in a sauté pan and sauté the onion and garlic until the onion turns translucent. Add bell pepper and mushrooms and cook for another 5 minutes. Pour into a colander and drain any liquid off the mixture.

In a mixing bowl, place three-quarters of the tomatoes, the olives, half of the feta cheese, half of the spinach, and half of the drained vegetable mixture. Toss until fully blended. Crack 4 eggs into a separate bowl and add the fresh herbs, salt, milk, and water. Beat this mixture until it is light and fluffy. Spoon half of the vegetable mixture into the piecrust and then pour half of the egg mixture over the vegetables. Repeat layers with the remaining vegetables and remaining egg mixture.

Cut the remaining cherry tomatoes in half. Scatter them, along with the rest of the feta cheese, over the top of the quiche. In the center of the quiche, crack the remaining egg on top of everything. Bake in a preheated oven at 375 degrees F for 45 minutes or until the filling is set and a knife inserted in the center comes out clean. Let quiche cool and set up for 15 minutes before serving.

DINNERS

Chicken Enchiladas with New Mexico Ranchero Sauce | 82

Chicken in a Basket | 85

Jaelitza's Sesame Chicken | 89

Southern Baked Chicken | 90

Torino Hazelnut Polenta | 91

Lamb Ratatouille with Creamy Polenta | 92

South Moroccan Lamb Couscous Tagine | 95

Grandma's German Goulash | 97

Rachel's Meat Loaf | 98

Asparagus & Shiitake Mushroom Strudel | 101

Milan-Style Lasagna | 102

Pad Thai Noodles | 105

Cashew & Rice Veggie Loaf | 107

Quinoa & Veggie Soufflé | 109

Aubergine (Eggplant) Niçoise | 110

Spinach-Potato Roulade | 112

Green Tea– & Miso–Glazed Tempeh | 115

Shiitake Mushroom Vegetable Cakes | 116

Blackened Catfish | 117

Grilled Catfish Burrito | 118

Crab Cakes | 120

Ginger-Glazed Salmon | 122

South Indian Coconut Chicken Curry | 124

Smoked Salmon Spanakopita | 127

VEGETARIAN VERSION

To make a vegetarian version of this dish, eliminate the chicken and replace the chicken stock in the Ranchero Sauce with vegetable stock or water. If you like, you can replace the chicken with any combination of the following: diced and sautéed potatoes, sweet potatoes, butternut squash, or green or yellow zucchini. You can also add fresh or frozen corn and crumbled tempeh or tofu. To make a vegan version, eliminate the cheese as well.

The Esalen kitchen is unique because two-thirds of its staff are students, most working in the kitchen for only one month. Some stay for as long as one year. This recipe comes from one of our students, Denise Ladwig, from New Mexico. She became both a baker and a cook during her stay and brought some of her New Mexican culture with her, as you can taste in this recipe.

Serves 4 to 6

ENCHILADAS

   2 pounds chicken breasts
   1 medium yellow onion, quartered
   1 tablespoon Mexican oregano or marjoram
   2 teaspoons sea salt
   3 quarts water
 12 corn tortillas
   1 pound Monterey Jack cheese, grated
   1 medium yellow onion, minced
$1/2$ pound of queso fresco or soft goat cheese
   2 tablespoons chopped cilantro
   1 recipe Ranchero Sauce (see page 180)

Continued on page 84

*Chicken Enchiladas with
New Mexico Ranchero Sauce*

CORN TORTILLAS

Choosing good quality corn tortillas is important for the best flavor in your enchiladas. Look for freshly made tortillas and those with simple ingredients such as corn, water, lime, and salt. Thicker corn tortillas rather than paper-thin ones usually have a better flavor and more closely resemble homemade.

Boil chicken breasts, quartered onions, Mexican oregano or marjoram, and salt in 3 quarts of water for about 20 minutes or until chicken is done. Remove chicken and let cool, reserving the stock. Shred the chicken when cooled. Lightly oil a 9- x 9-inch baking dish with vegetable oil.

Dip the tortillas into the Ranchero Sauce and lay on a flat surface. Fill with about 1/12 of the Jack cheese, 1/12 of the shredded chicken, and a bit of the minced onion. Roll up in a cylinder shape and place in the baking dish. When all 12 tortillas have been rolled, pour some of the remaining sauce over the enchiladas and sprinkle the queso fresco or goat cheese over the top. Bake in a preheated oven at 350 degrees F for 20 minutes. Remove from oven and sprinkle cilantro over the top before serving.

CHICKEN IN A BASKET

This elegant dish, served in a basket of puff pastry, is sure to impress family and friends. The chicken is also wonderful served over rice or pasta. Marion Cascio brought this dish to our kitchen. It was one that she prepared many times in her family restaurant.

Serves 6 to 8

STOCK

1	tablespoon vegetable oil
1/2	medium yellow onion, chopped into 1-inch dice
8	cups water
1	whole chicken
3	tablespoons dry sage
2	bay leaves
1 1/2	tablespoons sea salt
2	medium carrots, split in half lengthwise
2	stalks celery, cut in 2-inch pieces

Place the oil and onion in a 6- to 8-quart saucepan over medium-high heat and sauté onion until it's translucent, about 3 minutes. Add the water, chicken, herbs, salt, and remaining vegetables. Raise the heat to high and bring the stock to a boil, and then reduce heat to a simmer and cover. Cook until the leg of the chicken comes out easily from the rest of the chicken and the stock has a rich smell.

Remove chicken from pot with a pair of tongs or a large slotted spoon and put it on a plate to cool. Strain the stock and discard the other ingredients. Let stock cool; skim off the fat and reserve it for the cream sauce.

Continued on page 86

MAKING A PUFF PASTRY BASKET

You will need 1 box puff pastry (1 pound). Cut a sheet of puff pastry into 4 equal squares. Put the dough in front of you in a diamond shape. Place the corner closest to you against the corner farthest away from you, forming a triangle. Leave a 1/2-inch border along the edge and cut the triangle on two sides. Don't connect the two sides. Open the pastry so it has its diamond shape, and moisten the edges with water. Pick up one of the cut corners and flip it to the other side. Take the opposite corner and flip it over to the other side. Repeat this process for each puff pastry basket.

Place pastry on a baking sheet that has been covered with parchment paper and bake in a preheated oven at 350 degrees F for 15 minutes or until the pastry is golden brown. Take out of oven and let cool for 5 minutes, and then press the center down with a spoon to form a basket. Place the basket on a plate and ladle the cream chicken into the basket until it's full.

CREAM SAUCE

$\frac{1}{2}$ cup chicken fat skimmed from top of stock

$\frac{1}{2}$ cup unsalted butter, melted

$1\frac{1}{2}$ cups unbleached all-purpose flour

6 cups chicken stock, cooled

1 cup half-and-half or heavy cream

Start by making a roux: Pour the chicken fat and butter into a large saucepan and put over medium heat for a few minutes; then add the flour to the hot fat, stirring constantly using a wire whisk. Continue to stir so the roux doesn't burn; if it starts to smoke, remove it from the heat for a minute. Whisk the roux for about 5 minutes, and then stir in the stock and cream. Raise the heat and bring the sauce to a boil, and then turn off heat and set sauce aside.

FILLING

1 pound asparagus

$\frac{1}{2}$ pound snow peas

$\frac{1}{2}$ pound button mushrooms

Cooked chicken from stock

Juice of $1\frac{1}{2}$ lemons

Sea salt to taste

$\frac{1}{4}$ teaspoon black pepper

Chopped fresh parsley for garnish

Trim the bottoms of the asparagus, and then cut asparagus into 1/2-inch pieces. Place in a steamer and steam for about 8 minutes or until the asparagus is tender but slightly crunchy. Peel the strings off the peas, and then cut peas in half. Wipe the mushrooms clean and cut into quarters.

Remove the skin from the cooked chicken and discard. Debone the meat and break into bite-size pieces. Add the vegetables and chicken to the cream sauce. Add the lemon juice, salt, and pepper. Turn up the heat and stir constantly as the sauce comes to a boil. Remove sauce from heat and garnish with parsley. Ladle into puff pastry baskets.

Jaelitza's Sesame Chicken

JAELITZA'S SESAME CHICKEN

Back in the late '70s, I was a staff cook at Esalen at the same time that Jaelitza was. Jaelitza had traveled the world in her youth, lived in Africa, and settled in California where she became a schoolteacher. She decided to change her life—she left her job and found her way to Esalen in the late '70s. She was on the Esalen cooking staff for many years.

Jaelitza was the Zen Buddhist mother superior of the Esalen kitchen. She did her job with skill, grace, and unnerving calm in the eye of the storm of chaos that was, at times, the Esalen kitchen. She exemplified to the work scholars love and caring for the tasks they performed. She pointed them to the moment-to-moment awareness of washing potatoes, chopping broccoli, or marinating chicken. And she had a Slavic heart that filled the kitchen with her overpowering loving presence.

Serves 4

- ¼ cup vegetable oil
- ¼ cup tamari soy sauce
- 2 tablespoons white wine
- 2 tablespoons honey
- 1 clove garlic
- ¼ teaspoon grated fresh ginger
- 1 teaspoon red chili flakes
- 3 tablespoons sesame seeds
- 1 whole chicken, cut in 8 pieces
- 1 medium yellow onion, cut in ½-inch dice

Mix the oil, soy sauce, wine, and honey in a small bowl until well blended. Mince the garlic and add it to the marinade along with the ginger, chili flakes, and sesame seeds.

Place a ladleful of the marinade in a baking dish. Don't use a large baking dish; the chicken should fit in snugly. Lay the chicken pieces in the dish skin-side up, and then ladle the rest of the marinade over the chicken. Marinate at least 1/2 hour before cooking. It helps to prick the chicken pieces with a meat fork so that the marinade can be absorbed into the meat.

Bake in a preheated oven at 350 degrees F for about 1 hour total, covering it only for the first 20 minutes. After 20 minutes, remove cover, baste, and bake 20 minutes more. Then baste again and sprinkle with chopped onion. Return to oven for final 20 minutes of baking. The chicken will develop its own juice that will blend nicely with the marinade. The meat will turn a beautiful barbecued brown. It is done when the interior temperature of the meat reaches 165 degrees F on a meat thermometer.

SOUTHERN BAKED CHICKEN

This is a healthy way to have crisp, crunchy fried chicken without the extra fat from the frying, and the crisp crust clings to the chicken without flaking off like some of the greasier fried chicken recipes. And there is no messy hot fat splattering everywhere!

Serves 4

- 1   cup almonds, finely ground
- 1   cup cashews, finely ground
- 3   cups Rice Crispies, finely ground
- 1   cup finely grated Parmesan or Asiago cheese
- 2   tablespoons Cajun Spice Blend (see page 117)
- 1   teaspoon dried oregano
- 2   teaspoons dried thyme
- 1   tablespoon dried basil
- $1/4$ teaspoon ground fennel seed
- 1   tablespoon paprika
- 1   tablespoon ground sage
- 1   teaspoon black pepper
- 1   teaspoon sea salt
- 1   teaspoon granulated garlic
- 1   chicken, cut into 8 pieces

The simplest way to grind the small quantity of nuts and Rice Crispies is in an electric seed grinder or coffee grinder. The cheese can be grated on the fine grate of a hand cheese grater.

Blend the nuts, Rice Crispies, cheese, and all the spices together until they are well mixed. Cover all sides of the chicken pieces with the breading mix, and then place them on a baking sheet. Bake in a preheated oven at 400 degrees F for 45 minutes. The best way I know to test the chicken for doneness is to place a thermometer into the meat. Chicken is done when it reaches 165 degrees F interior temperature.

The breading mix makes 5 cups and will keep for several weeks if sealed and refrigerated.

TORINO HAZELNUT POLENTA

The Piedmont region of northern Italy is famous for its hazelnuts. In the forests and orchards around Torino grow a variety of hazelnuts that have an exceptionally rich flavor. The nut has a reddish hue rather than a classical hazel color, and is more oblong than the classical round shape of most hazelnuts. These nuts have a fragrant taste that gives this regional dish its name.

Serves 4

- 1/2 cup sun-dried tomatoes
- 2 cups hazelnuts
- 3 cups vegetable stock or water
- 3 cups half-and-half or whole milk
- 1 1/2 teaspoons sea salt
- 1 teaspoon dry oregano
- 1 teaspoon dry basil
- 2 cups polenta
- 1 teaspoon minced garlic
- 3 green onions, trimmed and sliced into fine rounds
- 2 tablespoons butter
- 1 cup Parmesan or Asiago cheese, grated
- 1/2 cup fresh basil, finely chopped

Soak the tomatoes in warm water for 20 minutes. Place in a colander to drain and set aside. Roast the hazelnuts in a heavy-bottomed frying pan over medium heat until the skins began to crack. This is necessary because the dark brown skin is bitter and needs to be taken off. Keep stirring the nuts as you cook them, and roast until you see the skins start to crack and peel. Set aside and let cool. Once cool, rub the hazelnuts between your hands. Loosened skins will come away easily; some skins will remain, and that's fine. Chop the nuts into coarse, small chunks.

Oil an 8-inch baking dish. In a heavy-bottomed saucepan over high heat, combine the stock, milk, salt, oregano, and basil and bring to a boil. Be sure to stir so the milk doesn't scorch on the bottom. Whisk in the polenta in a slow and steady stream to keep any lumps from forming.

When all the polenta has been added to the liquid, lower the heat to medium and continue to stir for about 15 minutes, or more importantly, until the grains are soft and not gritty to the taste. When the polenta is soft, stir in the following ingredients in the order listed: garlic, green onions, drained sun-dried tomatoes, butter, cheese, half of the fresh basil, and half of the hazelnuts. Quickly pour the mixture into the oiled baking dish and then smooth out the top with a spatula. Sprinkle the remaining hazelnuts over the top of the polenta and gently press down with your hands to fix the nuts on the surface. Let the polenta rest and set up for about 15 minutes.

Cover and bake in a preheated oven at 350 degrees F for about 30 to 45 minutes or until the polenta pulls slightly away from the sides of the dish. Cut into serving-size pieces and serve topped with a Green Olive & Roasted Roma Tomato Sauce (see page 176). Sprinkle with the remaining fresh basil.

VEGAN OPTION

To make this recipe vegan, replace milk with soy milk and butter with margarine.

Lamb Ratatouille can be made into
a high-protein vegetarian/vegan dish
by replacing the lamb with 1 pound of
tofu or tempeh. Add the tofu or tempeh
at the same time you add the rest of
the vegetables.

LAMB RATATOUILLE WITH CREAMY POLENTA

After some research, we at the Esalen kitchen discovered the most natural meat came from animals that ate what the Creator had designed them to eat: grass. Grass-fed animals are not as common as one would think in today's markets. At the time I was in charge at the Esalen kitchen, we could only find New Zealand lamb to be guaranteed grass-fed. All other red meat on the market was corn-fed, grown organically or not. I think the situation has changed since then. Grass-fed red meat can be found in the market today. Ratatouille is the most famous Provencal vegetable dish, and in this recipe we've added tender juicy lamb. The lamb is permeated with the flavor of the Ratatouille while still remaining its own succulent flavor.

Serves 4 to 6

LAMB RATATOUILLE

- 1 tablespoon vegetable oil
- 1 pound lamb stew meat
- 1 large red onion, diced in 3/4-inch pieces
- 2 medium red bell peppers, diced in 3/4-inch pieces
- 2 medium green bell peppers, diced in 3/4-inch pieces
- 1 large eggplant, diced in 3/4-inch pieces
- 2 medium zucchini, diced in 3/4-inch pieces
- 2 cloves garlic, finely minced
- 3 tablespoons tomato paste
- 4 cups tomato sauce
- 1 tablespoon minced fresh rosemary
- 1 tablespoon minced fresh thyme
- 1 tablespoon sea salt
- 1 teaspoon black pepper
- 1 tablespoon minced fresh oregano
- 2 tablespoons minced fresh basil

Place the oil in an 8-quart heavy-bottomed saucepan over high heat. Once the oil is hot, drop in the lamb, searing on all sides until brown. Add the vegetables, tomato paste, tomato sauce, rosemary, thyme, salt, and pepper; cover and reduce heat to a simmer. Cook for 1½ to 2 hours or until the lamb is tender. Add the fresh oregano and basil 2 minutes before serving. This is best served over Creamy Polenta.

CREAMY POLENTA

- 2 tablespoons unsalted butter
- 1¼ teaspoons salt
- 4 cups milk
- ¾ cup polenta

In a 2-quart saucepan over high heat, add the butter, salt, and milk, and stir until the mixture boils. Slowly add the polenta to the milk as you briskly whisk the liquid. Lower the heat to a simmer and cook for 15 minutes, stirring often. Remove from heat and serve warm. Creamy Polenta is also excellent served with Grandma's German Goulash (see page 97).

VEGAN CREAMY POLENTA

Follow the same recipe for regular Creamy Polenta, but substitute soy milk for the milk and unhydrogenated vegetable margarine for the butter.

South Moroccan Lamb
Couscous Tagine

SOUTH MOROCCAN LAMB COUSCOUS TAGINE

This is the national dish of Morocco, Algeria, and Tunisia, which are located in the northwestern corner of Africa. I learned this recipe from a woman who came from the Atlas Mountains in southern Morocco. She, along with her husband and their two small children, was my neighbor when I lived just outside Marseilles, France. I remember the day I walked into their house and was fascinated by the sweet and pungent smells of Arab spices. I was also fascinated to see for the first time a family living without Western furniture. They ate sitting on cushions at a small table low to the floor. This dish is an exciting culinary experience that you'll want to share with friends.

Serves 6

- 1 small eggplant, peeled and cut into 1-inch cubes
- 1 onion, cut into 1-inch cubes
- 2 carrots, cut into 1-inch rounds
- 1 small celery root, turnip, or rutabaga, peeled and cut into 1-inch cubes
- 1 small yam, peeled and cut into 1-inch cubes
- 1 medium zucchini, cut into 1-inch rounds
- 1 quart vegetable stock or water
- 1 tablespoon sea salt
- 1 cinnamon stick
- 2 whole cloves
- 1 teaspoon cumin
- 1 teaspoon turmeric
- 1 pound lamb, cut into 1-inch cubes
- 2 medium Roma tomatoes, cut into 1-inch cubes
- ½ teaspoon saffron threads
- 2 cups cooked chickpeas
- 1 tablespoon fresh cilantro, finely chopped

Continued on next page

VEGETARIAN AND VEGAN OPTION

To make this into a vegetarian or vegan dish, eliminate the lamb. Instead use 1 pound of firm, well-drained tofu cut into 1-inch cubes. Sauté the tofu in the same order as the lamb, adding 1 tablespoon of toasted cumin to the tofu as you sauté it.

COOKING CHICKPEAS

I use the quick-soak method for cooking chickpeas. Check for any stones and remove them, then place chickpeas in a saucepan and cover with 3 times the water. Bring to a boil, and then turn off the heat and let chickpeas sit, covered, for 1 hour. Drain off the water and rinse the beans well. Discard this cooking water.

Transfer them to a 2-quart saucepan with 6 cups water and cook over high heat. Add 1 tablespoon each of dry sage, oregano, thyme, and sea salt to the cooking water. Cook until the beans are tender, about 1 hour.

Save the cooking water to use as vegetable stock for the South Moroccan Lamb Couscous Tagine. Cooking chickpeas using this method gives the beans a more robust flavor.

COOKING COUSCOUS

Couscous is semolina wheat that has been presteamed. Cooking couscous is not necessary; all that is needed is to rehydrate the grain. To make 4 servings, place 2 cups of dry couscous into a bowl with 1 tablespoon of olive oil. Rub the oil into the couscous by rubbing the grain between your hands. The grain will turn a shade darker when the olive oil has been rubbed in properly. Pour boiling water to about 1/4 inch over the grain and cover with a very tight seal such as a tight-fitting lid or aluminum foil. Leave for 20 minutes, uncover, and fluff the couscous by lightly scraping it with a fork.

In a heavy skillet over high heat, sear each vegetable, except the tomatoes, separately for about 4 minutes each. Place the vegetables, except the tomatoes, in a 6-quart saucepan over high heat, and add the vegetable stock, salt, cinnamon stick, cloves, cumin, and turmeric. When it comes to a boil, lower the heat to simmer and cover. Let the stew simmer for 1 hour or until the vegetables are half cooked.

After about 1 hour sear the lamb in the heavy skillet, cooking until browned, about 4 to 5 minutes. Add it to the saucepan along with the tomatoes. Bring to a boil again, and then lower the heat to simmer for another 1/2 hour.

Dry-toast the saffron in a small skillet over a low heat, stirring so it does not burn. The smell of the saffron will perfume the air. Stir the saffron into the stew along with the chickpeas and cook until the vegetables are done, about another 10 minutes. Add the fresh cilantro just before serving. This dish is traditionally ladled over a bed of cooked couscous.

GRANDMA'S GERMAN GOULASH

Goulash originated in Hungary and is traditionally a meat stew made with onions; its main seasoning is paprika—Hungarian paprika to be exact! Goulash is a common dish in many of the eastern European countries. This recipe comes from Marion Cascio's East German grandmother. She remembers her Oma AnaLiza cooking this recipe, using wild boar meat instead of the traditional beef.

Serves 6 to 8

2	tablespoons vegetable oil
1 1/2	pounds beef stew meat, cut into 1-inch cubes
2	large yellow onions, cut in 1/2-inch half moons
2	large red bell peppers, cut in 1/2-inch cubes
2	large green bell peppers, cut in 1/2-inch cubes
2	tablespoons tomato paste
1	tablespoon Hungarian paprika
1 1/3	tablespoons sea salt
2	bay leaves
1/2	teaspoon freshly ground black pepper
3/4	cup water

Preheat a heavy-bottomed 6-quart saucepan or cast-iron Dutch oven, and then add the oil and meat. Brown meat on all sides over high heat. Add the onions and lower the heat to medium. The meat absorbs the flavor of the onions as they sauté together. Cook this mixture for 1/2 hour or until the onions have fully caramelized.

Add the bell peppers, tomato paste, paprika, salt, bay leaves, pepper, and water. Raise the heat and bring the goulash to a boil; then lower the heat to a simmer and cover. Let the goulash simmer for 1 1/2 hours or until the meat is soft and tender. The goulash is best served over Creamy Polenta (see page 93). Add 1 teaspoon of chopped fresh rosemary just before serving.

Marion Cascio, Tina Wehr, and Andy Glazer

VEGETARIAN AND VEGAN VERSION

To make this version, eliminate the beef. Start by caramelizing the onion in the vegetable oil, and then add the bell peppers and cook together for 15 minutes. Add the tomato paste, 2 cups of tomato sauce, 1/2 pound tempeh, and the paprika, salt, bay leaves, pepper, and water. Bring to a boil and let cook for 20 minutes. Serve over Creamy Polenta (see page 93). Add 1 teaspoon of chopped fresh rosemary just before serving.

RACHEL'S MEAT LOAF

Rachel Fann has the mother role in the Esalen kitchen. I've witnessed her transform many a work scholar with her motherly love. When asked to describe her thoughts about cooking at Esalen, Rachel said: "Whether I'm scooping out cocoa to make hot chocolate or mixing up my meat loaf, I think of those I'm cooking for as my own family. I will be forever grateful for this work, for the deep peacefulness I feel, even in the middle of all the chaos. This is my work in the world, to love others through my cooking."

Rachel Fann

Serves 8

- 2 teaspoons vegetable oil
- 1 medium yellow onion, finely diced
- 1 stalks finely diced celery
- 2 pounds ground beef
- 2 eggs
- ¼ cup Worcestershire sauce
- 1 cup bread crumbs
- 1 tablespoon sea salt
- 1 tablespoon freshly ground black pepper
- 1 (16-ounce) can tomato sauce

In a skillet over medium heat, sauté the onion in the vegetable oil until translucent. Add the celery and sauté until celery is tender and the onions take on a golden appearance.

Place the meat in a mixing bowl; beat the egg and blend into the meat. Add the Worcestershire sauce, bread crumbs, sautéed vegetables, salt, and pepper and mix all of this until well blended. Place the meat loaf on a sheet of parchment paper and shape into the loaf shape; then wrap the meat loaf in the parchment paper. This will keep it from drying out in the oven. Place in an oven preheated to 350 degrees F and bake for 1 hour. Unwrap the meat loaf, pour the tomato sauce over the top, and place back into the oven uncovered for another 20 to 30 minutes or until the meat loaf is firm and evenly brown. A meat thermometer should read 165 degrees F when it is done.

*Asparagus & Shiitake
Mushroom Strudel*

ASPARAGUS & SHIITAKE MUSHROOM STRUDEL

This is an elegant vegetarian dish that we served often at Esalen while I managed the kitchen. This recipe originated on the shores of Lake Constance, where the countries of Germany, Austria, and Switzerland share a border. This dish is usually served at Esalen with Porcini Mushroom Sauce (see page 177).

Serves 4 to 6

    1   tablespoon vegetable oil
    1   medium yellow onion, cut in $^1/_2$-inch dice
  $^1/_2$ pound shiitake mushrooms, cut in $^1/_2$-inch pieces
  $^1/_4$ pound button mushrooms, cut in $^1/_2$-inch pieces
    1   pound asparagus
   12   ounces ricotta cheese
    1   cup grated Asiago cheese
    3   tablespoons chopped parsley
  $^1/_2$ teaspoon freshly ground black pepper
    1   tablespoon salt
    1   (1-pound) box puff pastry (2 sheets)

Heat the oil in a sauté pan over high heat, add the onion, and sauté until golden brown. Add the mushrooms to the onions, lower the heat to medium, and cook another 8 minutes. Trim the asparagus stalks, and then cut asparagus into 1/2-inch pieces and steam for 5 minutes or until the stalks feel tender, but slightly crunchy.

Place the onions, mushrooms, and asparagus in a mixing bowl and add the ricotta, Asiago, parsley, pepper, and salt. Mix until everything is blended.

On a lightly floured surface, roll out one sheet of the pastry dough to a 9- x 11-inch rectangle. Fold the rolled dough into fourths and lay it on a clean kitchen towel that is bigger than the unfolded dough. Unfold the dough onto the towel. On the third of the dough that is closest to you, place half of the filling, leaving a 1-inch border along all edges. Lightly wet the upper edge of the pastry dough with water. Roll the strudel away from you in a tube or jellyroll shape. Continue to roll until you have reached the wet edge and pat the seam with your hands until the strudel sticks together. Fold the ends and press to seal them. Repeat for the second sheet of pastry dough and the remaining half of the filling.

Take both ends of the kitchen towel and gently roll the strudel off the towel and onto a baking pan lined with parchment paper. Bake in a preheated oven at 350 degrees F for 40 minutes. Remove from oven, slice, and serve. This recipe will make 2 strudels.

CASHEW MILK

To make Cashew Milk, finely grind 3 cups unsalted cashew pieces in a food processor, seed grinder, or coffee grinder. In a blender, put 1 cup hot tap water, 1 cup finely ground cashews, and a pinch of salt. Blend on high speed until it is silky smooth. Repeat two more times. This should be about 3 loads in the blender of water and finely ground nuts and should yield about 4 cups Cashew Milk. Add 1/4 teaspoon nutmeg to the cashew milk.

MILAN-STYLE LASAGNA

Northern Italian–style lasagna often has a white cream sauce instead of the classic tomato base sauce used in most Italian-style lasagnas. This recipe makes an elegant lasagna that can be served for a special occasion or an informal dinner. We replaced the béchamel sauce called for in the original recipe with a creamy cashew milk sauce that adds a very delicate flavor to this popular dish.

Serves 4 to 6

- 3 tablespoons olive oil
- 1 large yellow onion, cut into $1/2$-inch dice
- 3 medium carrots, finely grated
- 4 medium zucchini, finely grated
- 1 (16-ounce can) tomato sauce
- 1 (16-ounce can) diced tomatoes
- 2 tablespoons chopped fresh basil
- 3 teaspoons sea salt, divided
- 1 pound spinach or Swiss chard leaf, cut into $1/4$-inch ribbons
- 1 pound ricotta cheese
- 1 tablespoon chopped fresh oregano
- $1/2$ teaspoon freshly ground white pepper
- 12 lasagna noodles
- 1 recipe Cashew Milk (see sidebar)
- 2 cups grated Parmesan or Asiago cheese
- $1/2$ cup pumpkin seeds
- 2 teaspoons minced garlic

Place 1 tablespoon oil and the diced onion in a heavy-bottomed skillet over high heat for 3 minutes, add garlic and sauté until onion turns translucent. Transfer to a colander and drain. Using the same method, separately sauté the carrots and zucchini for about 5 minutes each, and then place in the colander with the onions. Add the tomato sauce, diced tomatoes, basil, and 2 teaspoons salt to the vegetables and mix.

Sauté spinach or chard until the bright green color starts to darken, about 5 minutes, and then drain in a wire strainer. Put the spinach or chard in a clean kitchen towel and press out as much water as possible. In a separate bowl, mix together the ricotta, chard, oregano, pepper, and 1 teaspoon of salt. Place the lasagna noodles in a pan and cover with hot tap water for 15 minutes, being sure that the noodles are not sticking to one another. Place noodles on a kitchen towel and dry thoroughly.

Cover the bottom of a 9- x 9-inch baking dish with a thin layer of Cashew Milk. Coat both sides of 4 lasagna noodles with Cashew Milk and lay in the bottom of the baking dish. Spread half of the carrot, zucchini, and onion mixture over the noodles, followed by one third of the cheese, and then half of the ricotta-chard mix. Spread a spoonful of the Cashew Milk over this. Repeat layers, ending with a layer of 4 coated lasagna noodles.

Spread the remaining Cashew Milk over the top layer of noodles and sprinkle the remaining one-third of the cheese over the top. Sprinkle the pumpkin seeds over the top of the cheese. Cover and bake in a preheated oven at 350 degrees F for 20 minutes, and then uncover and return to the oven for another 40 minutes. Remove from oven and let set up for about 10 minutes before serving.

Pad Thai Noodles

PAD THAI NOODLES

This recipe came out of a Staff Week dinner. Staff Week is when Esalen closes for a 5-day period during the Christmas holidays. Only employees and residents are allowed to be on the Esalen grounds. For this period, Esalen really lives as a community or small village. Each evening, a different department cooks dinner. One year the office decided to do a Thai menu. Shelton Phillips, one of the office staff, had been a guide in Thailand for eight years and learned this recipe while there. Of the many different versions of Pad Thais, this was his favorite.

Serves 4

NOODLES

- $1/2$ pound wide rice noodles, uncooked
- 2 eggs
- 3 teaspoons grated fresh ginger, divided
- 1 medium carrot, cut into $1/8$-inch pieces
- 3 teaspoons minced garlic, divided
- $1/4$ teaspoon sea salt
- 1 tablespoon water
- 2 tablespoons vegetable oil, divided
- 1 small red bell pepper, cut into $1/2$-inch dice
- 3 green onions, chopped in fine rounds
- $1/4$ pound mung bean sprouts, rinsed and drained
- $3/4$ cup whole dry-roasted peanuts
- 1 tablespoon chopped cilantro
  Juice of $1/2$ lime

Soak the rice noodles in hot tap water for about 15 minutes. They should be soft but not completely tender. Drain and set aside.

Beat the eggs in a bowl with 1 teaspoon of the ginger, 1 teaspoon of the garlic, the salt, and the water. Pour 1 tablespoon of the oil into a wok or heavy-bottomed skillet and set over medium heat. When the pan is heated, pour in the egg and scramble until well cooked. Once cooked, crumble eggs into bite-size pieces, and then set aside.

Over high heat, place the remaining tablespoon of oil into the wok or large heavy-bottomed skillet; add the remaining ginger and garlic, the carrot, and the bell pepper.

Stir-fry for a few minutes, and then add the green onions, bean sprouts, and peanuts. Continue to stir-fry for a few minutes more until the sprouts look limp. Stir in the noodles and scrambled egg and toss together with the vegetables for a minute more. Pour on the sauce and toss everything until it is lightly coated. Spoon the Pad Thai into a serving dish, garnish with the cilantro, and squeeze the juice of 1/2 lime over the dish. Serve immediately.

Continued on next page

ADDING PROTEIN

This recipe is a base for Pad Thai Noodles. If you want more protein, you can add tofu, fish and seafood, or chicken breast to the ingredients list. Add about 1 pound of the protein, cut in bite-size pieces. Precook the fish and chicken and add the protein at the beginning of stir-frying along with the carrots.

SAUCE

- $1/4$ cup tamari soy sauce
- 5 tablespoons Mirin rice wine
- 1 tablespoon rice vinegar
- 1 tablespoon toasted sesame oil
- $1/4$ cup coconut milk
  Juice of $1/2$ lime
- 2 tablespoons tamarind paste (optional)
- 3 tablespoons honey
- 1 teaspoon cayenne pepper
- $1/4$ cup crunchy peanut butter (use a good quality made from peanuts only)

Place in a blender the soy sauce, wine, vinegar, oil, coconut milk, and lime juice and blend. Add the tamarind paste if using, honey, cayenne, and peanut butter while the blender is running. Blend until smooth.

This sauce has to be one of the most unique Thai sauces that I've encountered.

CASHEW & RICE VEGGIE LOAF

This recipe is a great way of using up leftover rice. The veggie loaf has a dense, meaty texture and a hearty meat flavor. At Esalen, we serve this as the optional vegetarian main dish when Rachel's famous meat loaf is on the menu.

Serves 6

- 1 cup cooked short-grain brown rice
- 2 cups cashews
- 1 large yellow onion, coarsely chopped
- 2 teaspoons chopped garlic
- 1¼ cups minced crimini mushrooms
- 1 tablespoon minced fresh parsley
- 1 teaspoon minced fresh oregano
- 1 teaspoon minced fresh thyme
- 2 large pieces dried porcini mushrooms
- 2 eggs
- ½ cup ricotta or cottage cheese
- ½ teaspoon sea salt
- ¼ teaspoon cayenne pepper
- 1 tablespoon nutritional food yeast
- 2 cups finely grated Parmesan or Asiago cheese

Roast the cashews in the oven at 350 degrees F for 5 minutes, and then pulse the nuts in a food processor until finely chopped, or chop them by hand. In a sauté pan, sauté the onion in a small amount of vegetable oil over medium heat until translucent. Add the garlic, crimini mushrooms, and fresh herbs and sauté until the liquid has evaporated from the pan. Set this aside and let cool.

Grind the dry porcini in a seed grinder or coffee grinder. This should yield 2 teaspoons of fine powder. Beat the eggs with the ricotta, salt, cayenne, yeast, and porcini powder. In a mixing bowl, place the rice, nuts, egg mixture, cheese, and the cooked veggies.

Lightly oil a bread pan and line the bottom with parchment paper. Place the mixture in the pan, smooth with a spatula, and bake in the oven at 350 degrees F for 1 hour. The top should turn golden brown and a knife inserted in the loaf should come out clean. Let the loaf cool and set up in the pan for 10 minutes, and then slip it out of the pan and take off the parchment paper before placing it on a serving plate.

Quinoa & Veggie Soufflé

QUINOA & VEGGIE SOUFFLÉ

Quinoa has the highest protein content of any grain and is extremely rich in calcium. It was the basic staple of the Inca civilization and had been cultivated for over 3,000 years. In this recipe we have combined this nutritious grain with fresh vegetables and herbs and baked it with eggs and cheese to create a light and tasty soufflé.

Serves 4

3/4	cup quinoa
1 1/2	cups water
3	tablespoons oil, divided
2 1/2	cups grated carrots
1 1/2	teaspoons dried thyme, divided
2 1/2	cups grated zucchini
1	medium yellow onion, diced into 1/2-inch pieces
1	cup grated Asiago cheese
2	cups ricotta cheese
1 1/2	tablespoons sea salt
1/2	teaspoon pepper
2	tablespoons chopped fresh basil
4	eggs, separated

Place the quinoa in a fine sieve and rinse. In a saucepan over high heat, stir in the quinoa. Continue to stir 5 minutes or until it has a nutty aroma. Add the water, lower the heat to simmer, cover, and cook for 10 minutes. Set aside to cool.

In a sauté pan, add 1 tablespoon of oil and sauté the grated carrots with 1/2 teaspoon dried thyme. Set aside. Sauté the zucchini and onion separately, using the same method as the carrots. Place the quinoa, carrots, zucchini, and onion in a mixing bowl. Add the Asiago and ricotta and stir well. Add the salt, pepper, and basil. Beat the egg yokes and stir into the mixture, making sure everything is well mixed. Beat the egg whites until they have stiff peaks, and then gently fold them into the mixture.

Oil a 6-inch soufflé pan and pour the mixture into it. Bake in a preheated oven at 350 degrees F, covered, for 30 minutes; uncover and bake 30 minutes more. The soufflé is done when a knife inserted into it comes out clean.

AUBERGINE (EGGPLANT) NIÇOISE

In northern Italy, there are almost as many variations of Eggplant Parmesan as there are villages. Although the city of Nice is in France, at one time it was part of a vast empire that included the rest of northern Italy under the rule of the King of Savoy. This Nice version of Eggplant Parmesan is a lighter variation of the classic dish from Parma. It consists of many thin slices of eggplant that are lightly oiled. When baked, the multiple layers reduce down and develop a savory taste and a soft, chewy texture that is similar to veal.

Serves 4 to 6

3	eggplants
1	cup extra-virgin olive oil
2^{1}/$_{2}$	cups grated Parmesan or Asiago cheese
3	tablespoons chopped fresh basil

For this recipe, it is helpful to have a mandolin to slice the eggplants as thin as possible, but you can also use a knife.

With a vegetable peeler, peel the eggplants lengthwise in a stripe pattern by leaving a 1/2-inch gap of skin between each peeling. Slice the eggplants lengthwise from stem end to bottom. These slices should be as thin as possible. Dip both hands into the olive oil and hand-rub each slice of eggplant with a very light coating of oil. Redip your hands into the oil only after they become dry (approximately every 5 to 6 slices).

Cover the bottom of a well-oiled 9- x 11-inch baking dish with the oiled eggplant slices, making sure that the slices are touching but not overlapping. Sprinkle a thin layer of cheese over the top. Repeat with another layer of oiled eggplant followed by another layer of cheese, alternating the direction of the eggplant with each layer. Fill in any gaps between the slices with smaller pieces of eggplant so that the previous layer is completely covered. Continue layering until you reach a thickness of 2 inches, finishing with a thick layer of cheese.

Cover and place in a preheated oven at 350 degrees F for 45 minutes to 1 hour. It is done when you stick a fork into the eggplant and it gives like softened butter. Cut into slices and sprinkle with fresh basil. Serve with the Green Olive & Roasted Roma Tomato Sauce (see page 176).

SPINACH-POTATO ROULADE

This is an elegant vegetarian main dish that is fun and easy to prepare. The filling is full of tasty shiitake mushrooms and fresh spinach. It is rolled jellyroll style between a mashed potato base. At Esalen, we always serve it with Porcini Mushroom Sauce (see page 177).

Serves 4 to 6

ROULADE BASE

1 1/2	pounds russet potatoes
2 1/2	cups grated Parmesan cheese
1/4	cup olive oil
3	tablespoons finely chopped fresh basil
3	tablespoons soy bacon bits
1/4	teaspoon sea salt
	Pinch ground white pepper

Place potatoes, with skin on, in a saucepan and cover with water. Bring to a boil over medium-high heat. Lower to a simmer and cook until potatoes are soft enough to mash but still hold their firmness. Drain potatoes, place into a mixing bowl, and mash while still hot. Mash until they are smooth but stiff; don't over-mash. Stir in the cheese, oil, basil, bacon bits, salt, and pepper.

FILLING

2	medium yellow onions
	Olive oil
1/2	pound shiitake mushrooms
2	pounds fresh spinach or 1 pound frozen spinach, defrosted
2	cups ricotta cheese
	Pinch salt

ADDING PROTEIN

This recipe can be made into a meat dish by adding 1/2 pound of thinly sliced Parma ham. After you have spread out the potato mixture, layer the potatoes with the slices of ham before you place the filling on top. Roll, bake, and slice as per the recipe instructions.

The filling should be made while the potatoes are cooking. It is important to have the filling ready when you start to mash the potatoes. The potatoes should be warm so that they roll more easily.

Peel the onions and chop into half-moons. Preheat a small amount of oil in a sauté pan over high heat, add the onions and sauté until they turn golden brown, and then set aside. Chop the mushrooms into quarters and sauté in a small amount of oil until the water has evaporated from the pan. Mix with onions.

If you're using fresh spinach, remove the stems and chop leaves into 1/2-inch ribbons. With a small amount of oil, sauté the spinach until it wilts, then place in a strainer and drain off all water. If you're using frozen spinach, defrost and then place in strainer and press out as much water as possible. The vegetables in the roulade filling need to be as dry as possible.

Add the spinach to the onion and mushroom mixture, and then add the cheese and salt. Mix this well. Take a clean kitchen towel or a piece of 8- x 8-inch parchment paper. With a spatula, spread the hot potato mixture 1 inch thick onto the towel. Spread the filling evenly over the potato mixture. Gently lift the 2 corners nearest to you and slowly roll the roulade away from you. Roll into a tight roll, similar to a jellyroll. Then carefully take all 4 corners of the towel, and lift the roulade onto a baking sheet covered with parchment paper; roll the roulade off the towel as gently as possible. It should roll off without any trouble.

Brush the sides and top of the roulade with a light coating of olive oil and bake in a preheated oven at 350 degrees F for about 25 minutes or until the roulade is golden brown. Slice and serve hot with Porcini Mushroom Sauce (see page 177). The best way I have found to slice the roulade is with an electric knife; if this is not available, use a serrated knife. Have a serving spatula ready to catch the slice when it is cut free from the roulade.

Green Tea– & Miso–Glazed
Tempeh

GREEN TEA– & MISO–GLAZED TEMPEH

This recipe is one of the favorite ways we like to pre-pare tempeh in the Esalen kitchen. Tempeh is a low-fat, high-protein (30 percent) soy product from Indonesia. When cooked properly it has a moist, chicken-like flavor. Baking it in a green jasmine tea and white miso gives the tempeh a sweet-and-salty flavor with a hint of jasmine. This recipe was created by Jason Brodsky in the Esalen kitchen.

Serves 4

- 1 cup white mellow miso
- 1/2 cup maple syrup
- 2 tablespoons Mirin (rice cooking wine)
- 1 tablespoon roasted sesame oil
- 1 pound tempeh
- 4 bags jasmine green tea
- 1 cup boiling water
- 1 lemon, sliced into 1/4-inch rounds
- 1 tablespoon black sesame seeds
- 1 tablespoon brown sesame seeds
- 3 green onions, sliced into fine rounds

Whisk the miso, maple syrup, Mirin, and oil together ion a bowl until you have a smooth consistency and a sweet-salty taste that is unique to the miso and maple. Cut the tempeh into 4 cutlets and place them in an 8- x 8-inch baking dish; spoon a 1/4-inch layer of the miso-maple glaze on top. (Be sure to leave 1/4 cup of the glaze in the bowl.)

Place the tea bags into the bowl with the remaining glaze and pour the boiling water over the top. Let this brew for 5 minutes. You now have a miso and jasmine green tea. Carefully ladle this tea into the pan with the tempeh until it is just about halfway up the sides of the tempeh. Be careful not to disturb the glaze on top of the tempeh.

Place a lemon round on each tempeh cutlet and sprinkle the sesame seeds over the top. Cover the pan and place in a pre-heated oven at 350 degrees F for 30 minutes. Uncover and bake for another 15 minutes or until the glaze looks caramelized and somewhat dry. Sprinkle the green onions over the tempeh just before serving.

TOFU VERSION

This dish can also be prepared with tofu. Replace the tempeh with 1 pound of tofu. Slice the tofu into 4 cutlets and lay out on a kitchen towel that has been folded several times. Place another folded kitchen, on top of the tofu and press with your hand until as much water as possible has been removed from the tofu. Follow the instructions for the remainder of the recipe.

SHIITAKE MUSHROOM VEGETABLE CAKES

When we serve meat or fish as our main dinner course at Esalen, we always offer a vegetarian alternative. This recipe is served to our vegetarian guests when we have crab cakes on the menu. It's a wonderful dish loaded with creamy pine nuts and meaty-tasting shiitake mushrooms.

Serves 4

- 1 cup pine nuts
- 1 cup cooked couscous (see page 96)
- 1 tablespoon olive oil
- 1 large yellow onion, minced
- 2 teaspoons minced garlic
- 1/4 pound shiitake mushrooms, finely chopped
- 1 tablespoon finely chopped fresh parsley
- 1 tablespoon finely chopped fresh basil
- 1 teaspoon finely chopped fresh oregano
- 2 eggs
- 1/2 cup ricotta cheese
- 1 1/2 cups finely grated Parmesan or Asiago cheese
- 2 teaspoons ground dry porcini mushrooms
- 2 tablespoons nutritional food yeast
- 1/2 teaspoon sea salt
- 1/4 teaspoon cayenne pepper

Place the pine nuts on a baking sheet and toast in a preheated oven at 400 degrees F for 5 minutes or until they start to turn a very light brown. Remove from oven and finely chop them in a food processor or seed grinder. Place ground nuts, along with the couscous, in a mixing bowl.

In a sauté pan over high heat, sauté onion with the olive oil until translucent; then add garlic, shiitake mushrooms, and fresh herbs. Lower the heat to medium and cook until all the moisture has evaporated. Set this mixture aside to cool.

Whisk the eggs, ricotta, Parmesan or Asiago, porcini powder, yeast, salt, and cayenne together in a bowl and add to the couscous and nuts. Pour in the cooled vegetables and mix well. Let this sit for about 1/2 hour in the fridge before cooking. The mix should have a consistency like thick paste.

Take a spoonful of the mix and shape with your hands into cakes, about 3 inches in diameter and 3/4 inch thick. The cakes can be baked in the oven at 350 degrees F for about 45 minutes or until golden brown. If you bake them, be sure to oil the baking sheet. Or they can be pan-fried in a heavy-bottomed skillet with a little oil. This takes about 4 minutes on each side over medium-high heat.

BLACKENED CATFISH

Hot red peppers have been a common seasoning in Cajun cooking since the French refugees, called Cajuns, were deported from Canada to the bayous around New Orleans. Peppers are like wine grapes; the soil where they are grown makes a big difference. Avery Island is in a bayou outside of New Orleans and the island is made of sodium chloride—salt. It's this salty soil that produces the special fiery taste of Tabasco sauce that can be found from the simplest to the most elaborate of Cajun and Creole cooking. This recipe uses Tabasco in a classic Louisiana manner to blacken catfish.

Serves 4

   2   cups tomato juice
   2   tablespoons Cajun Spice Blend (see sidebar)
   2   tablespoons Tabasco
 $^1/_2$ teaspoon sea salt
   4   catfish fillets ($^1/_2$ pound each)
 $^1/_2$ cup vegetable oil

Mix the juice, Cajun Spice Blend, hot sauce, and salt in a bowl big enough to hold the catfish. Prick the fish on both sides with a fork to help absorb the marinade. Place fish into marinade and let soak in the fridge for at least 2 hours. This is also the base for the Grilled Catfish Burrito recipe (see page 118) that we served at the Esalen dining lodge.

Heat the oil in a heavy-bottomed skillet over high heat; drop the fish into the pan and fry until golden brown (about 5 minutes). Flip the fillets and brown on the other side for about the same amount of time. Drain on paper towels to absorb any excess oil.

Note: If you really want a hot spicy catfish, baste the fish as it cooks with the leftover marinade.

CAJUN SPICE BLEND

   2   tablespoons paprika
   1   tablespoon oregano
   1   teaspoon cayenne pepper
   1   teaspoon freshly ground black pepper
   1   teaspoon freshly ground white pepper
   1   teaspoon garlic powder
   1   teaspoon sea salt

Blend all ingredients together and store in an air-tight container. This makes just over 1/4 cup of spice blend.

GRILLED CATFISH BURRITO

This is a complete Cajun meal rolled into a flour tortilla. The grilling gives it a crisp crunch that adds to the already Cajun flavors. Fill your taste buds with Louisiana love!

Serves 6

6   burrito-size flour tortillas
3   cups very finely shredded green cabbage
1¹/₂   cups cooked red kidney beans (or substitute canned)
1¹/₂   cups cooked brown rice
2   cups sharp cheddar cheese, grated
1¹/₂   pounds cooked Blackened Catfish fillets (see page 117)
1¹/₂   teaspoons pasilla chile powder
3   tablespoons chopped cilantro
Sea salt to taste

Place a tortilla on a flat work surface. Spread 1/2 cup of shredded cabbage over one-third of the tortilla. Spread approximately 4 tablespoons each of the cooked beans and cooked rice over the cabbage. Sprinkle the rice and beans with shredded cheese, and then place 1/6 of the fish over this mixture. Sprinkle 1/4 teaspoon of the chili powder, 1/2 tablespoon of cilantro, and a pinch of sea salt over the burrito filling.

Take the burrito into your two hands and fold in the ends of the burrito. Roll the tortilla away from you, tucking in the tortilla tightly and giving the burrito shape as you tuck. Tuck any loose ends into the burrito, and then finish the roll. Repeat for the remaining 5 burritos.

A charbroiler grill is a great way to grill this burrito. Slowly roll the burrito across the hot grill until it's crisp and toasted. If you don't have a grill, used a heavy-bottomed skillet with a small amount of vegetable oil over a high heat. Roll the burrito in the skillet until crisp and toasted.

CRAB CAKES

This is a really light and delicate cake with the sweet taste of crabmeat accompanied by the flavor of fresh herbs and ground rice cereal. It's excellent served with Chipotle Cream Sauce or a good tartar sauce. These crab cakes were brought to Esalen by John Blunt.

Makes 12 cakes

1/2	medium yellow onion, minced
2	medium carrots, minced
3	stalks celery, minced
3	teaspoons vegetable oil, divided
1	pound crabmeat
2	cups Rice Crispies
1/2	teaspoon sea salt
	Pinch ground white pepper
1	tablespoon chopped fresh basil
1	tablespoon chopped fresh parsley
4	eggs

Amanecer Eizner, Ben Reebs, and Genevieve Medow-Jenkins

In a food processor, separately mince the onion, carrots, and celery. Sauté each vegetable separately in 1 teaspoon of vegetable oil; cook until the water has evaporated from the vegetables. Place the vegetables in a colander to drain any excess moisture.

Take the crabmeat and squeeze out any excess liquid by placing it in a clean kitchen towel and pressing out as much moisture as possible. Place crabmeat in a mixing bowl and add the vegetables.

Put the Rice Crispies in a food processor, seed grinder, or coffee grinder, and grind until you have a course meal. This should yield about 1 cup. (If you can't find Rice Crispies, use bread crumbs instead.) Add this to the mixing bowl along with the salt, pepper, basil, and parsley. Stir until well blended.

Beat the eggs in a separate bowl and pour into the mix; stir well until blended. Let the mixture set for about 1/2 hour before cooking.

Place a small amount of oil in a heavy-bottomed skillet over medium-high heat. Scoop about 1/4 cup of the mixture into the skillet. With two forks, shape the crab cake into a patty, about 2 1/2 inches in diameter and 3/4 inch thick. You can do this by pushing down on the cake with one fork as you push in on the sides of the cake with the other fork. Fry until golden brown on one side, then flip and cook the other side in the same manner.

GINGER-GLAZED SALMON

At Esalen, we are fortunate to be near the fishing port of Monterey. Because of this, fresh fish is available year-round. When the Pacific Wild Salmon season opens, we try to serve this fresh wild delicacy once a week. Ginger-Glazed Salmon is a favorite recipe of the longtime Esalen staff. The glaze enhances the natural subtle flavor of the salmon without overpowering it. It actually seals in the exquisite taste that is a hallmark of wild salmon. Bill Schrier brought this recipe to Esalen.

Serves 4

- 1 1/2 pounds salmon fillets, skin on
- 1 cup tamari soy sauce
- 1 cup cream sherry
- 2 tablespoons grated fresh ginger
- 2 tablespoons minced garlic
- 3 tablespoons Sucanat (dehydrated cane juice) or brown sugar

Blend all ingredients except salmon in a saucepan and place over medium heat until sugar dissolves; then remove from heat. When the marinade cools, pour over salmon fillets and let the fish marinate for at least 2 hours.

At Esalen, we cook this recipe on the grill, but if that isn't a possibility, you can cook it in a skillet with a small amount of oil over medium-high heat. To cook on the grill, brush the flesh side with marinade and place salmon on the grill flesh side down. Cook for approximately 4 to 5 minutes, and then turn to brown the skin side for about the same amount of time. Brush the skin side with the remaining marinade before turning.

The way to know if the salmon is done is to touch it with your fingers. If the fish is done, it will have a firm feeling to the touch; if not it will still feel pulpy or mushy.

VEGETARIAN OPTION

We offer Ginger-Glazed Tofu Steaks as the vegetarian option at Esalen when we serve the salmon. Cut 1 pound of tofu into 4 steaks. Using a kitchen towel, press as much water out of the tofu as possible without breaking it apart. Prick the tofu with a fork and then marinate using the recipe above. Grill or pan-fry as above with the fish.

VEGETARIAN AND VEGAN VERSION

In the vegetarian and vegan version of this curry, the chicken breast is replaced by 1 pound of tofu. Start by getting out the excess moisture from the tofu. Cut the tofu into four 1/2-inch pieces and place on a clean folded kitchen towel. Place another folded towel on top of the tofu and put a plate on top. Take a heavy object and put it on the plate to make a press. Leave for 15 minutes or longer. Take the tofu out of the press and cut into 1-inch cubes. Place 1 tablespoon of oil in the sauté pan and sauté the tofu along with 1 teaspoon ground cumin until the tofu forms a brownish skin on its sides. Add the tofu to the curry when the cauliflower and zucchini are added.

Raj came to Esalen from Calcutta and worked in the Esalen kitchen as a work scholar. One day he came into my office and asked if he could make a dinner. He had a brother-in-law who was a chef in a posh hotel in Calcutta and he had gotten this recipe from him. I adapted the recipe to our kitchen, and on my next cooking shift we prepared this dish together. It was a delicious curry and many people came into the kitchen raving about how tasty the meal had been.

Serves 4 to 6

CURRY PASTE

 3 tablespoons good quality curry powder
 1 tablespoon garam masala
 1 tablespoon turmeric powder
 2 teaspoons black mustard seed
 2 teaspoons paprika
 1 1/2 teaspoons cumin
 1 1/4 teaspoons cinnamon
 1 teaspoon mustard powder
 1 teaspoon nutmeg
 1 teaspoon ginger powder
 1/2 teaspoon cayenne pepper (or more if desired)
 1/4 teaspoon clove powder
 1/4 teaspoon ground cardamom
 2 cups coconut milk (1 14-ounce can)

On low heat, dry roast all ingredients except coconut milk in a heavy-bottomed skillet (cast-iron is best). Roast until the bouquet of the spices becomes very strong and their color changes to a deeper hue. Be careful not to burn the spices. Put the spices in an 8-quart saucepan. Whisk in the coconut milk, stirring constantly and blending well with the spices. Simmer over low heat for 3 minutes.

CHICKEN

2	teaspoons sea salt, divided
1	pound skinless, boneless chicken breasts
3	tablespoons vegetable oil, divided
2	medium-size yellow onions, chopped into 1-inch dice
1½	cups chicken stock, vegetable stock, or water
2	carrots, cut into 1-inch rounds
1	medium-size yam, chopped into 1-inch dice
¼	pound button mushrooms
1	small head cauliflower
1	medium zucchini, cut into 1-inch rounds
1	tablespoon chopped cilantro
1	cup cashew nuts

Lightly salt each side of the chicken breast, and then place on a baking sheet and bake in a preheated oven at 350 degrees F for 10 minutes on each side; this will dry out and par-cook the chicken. Let chicken cool and then chop into 1-inch dice. Set aside.

Put 1 tablespoon vegetable oil into the same skillet that you roasted the spices in and sauté the onion in the oil over medium-high heat until translucent. Add to the curry paste along with the stock or water. Add 1 more tablespoon of vegetable oil to the skillet and sauté the carrots and yams over medium-high heat for about 3 minutes; add the mushrooms and sauté until the water has evaporated. Add these cooked vegetables to the curry sauce and raise the heat to medium until the sauce comes to a boil. Then lower the heat to a simmer and cover.

Continued on next page

DRIED FRUIT CHUTNEY

This chutney can be made with any dried
fruit. Experiment with different fruits and
find a favorite. The chutney will keep for
2 weeks in the fridge. This recipe uses
raisins.

   2 cups raisins
   3 tablespoons fresh lemon juice
   $1/4$ teaspoon cayenne pepper, or more
        according to taste
   2 tablespoons finely grated fresh
        ginger
   2 teaspoons minced garlic
   1 teaspoon sea salt
   2 teaspoons fresh cilantro

This recipe is easiest to make in a food
processor. It can also be made in a blender
or food mill. Add the raisins and lemon
juice and process into a smooth paste.
Then add the cayenne, ginger, garlic, and
salt and blend well. Garnish with chopped
cilantro.

Pour the remaining 1 tablespoon of oil into the skillet and sauté
the cauliflower for 3 minutes, and then add the zucchini and cook
for another 3 minutes. Set aside.

Bring curry back to a boil then reduce to a simmer. Simmer for
about 15 minutes and then add the chicken, zucchini, cauliflower,
and remaining salt. Simmer for another 30 minutes and then
remove from heat and stir in the cilantro.

Dry-roast cashews in a heavy-bottomed pan until they start to
turn a light brown. Pour curry mixture into serving bowl and
sprinkle cashews over the top. In the Esalen dining lodge, this dish
is normally served over brown basmati rice along with Cucumber
Raita Salad (see page 140) and raisin chutney.

SMOKED SALMON SPANAKOPITA

We transformed this classic Greek vegetarian dish to accommodate our guests who crave a little more animal protein in their diets. The smoky, savory flavor of the salmon gives an added layer of taste to the feta cheese and spinach nestled between the crisp layers of the filo dough.

Serves 6

- 1   medium yellow onion, cut into $1/2$-inch dice
- 2   tablespoons olive oil
- 2   pounds fresh spinach (or 2 frozen packages), stemmed and chopped
- $1^1/2$ cups crumbled feta cheese
- 2   teaspoons minced garlic
- $1/2$ cup ricotta cheese
- 2   eggs
- 1   teaspoon chopped fresh dill
- $1/4$ teaspoon cayenne pepper
- 2   teaspoons sea salt
- $1/2$ bunch parsley, finely chopped
- $1/2$ pound filo dough
- $1/2$ cup melted butter
- $1/2$ pound smoked salmon (thinly sliced lox)

Sauté the onion in the olive oil for 4 minutes or until it becomes translucent. Add the spinach and cook, stirring constantly until tender. If you use frozen spinach, defrost and squeeze out excess water before sautéing. Place in colander and drain thoroughly.

In a separate mixing bowl, mix the feta, garlic, ricotta, eggs, dill, cayenne, salt, and parsley until well blended. Add the well-drained spinach mixture.

Brush the bottom and sides of a 9- x 9-inch baking dish with melted butter. Cut the filo sheets to fit the baking dish. Lay out 1 sheet of filo at the bottom of the dish and brush with melted butter. Repeat this process with 4 additional sheets, brushing each lightly with butter before laying the next layer down. Using a spatula, spread a 1/2-inch layer of the spinach mixture evenly over the dough. Cover this mixture with a thin layer of smoked salmon.

Continue this layering process: After every 4 sheets of filo, spread the spinach mixture and then the salmon, and then continue with 4 more layers of filo until you run out of the spinach mixture and salmon. After the final layer has been spread, then continue layering the filo dough until you finish using all the dough. Remember you must brush each layer with butter and brush the top of the final layer.

Bake in a preheated oven at 350 degrees F for about 45 minutes or until the top is golden brown. Cut into squares and serve warm.

Note: Keep filo dough covered with a damp cloth or plastic wrap so that it does not dry out.

SALADS

Curried Chicken Salad | 130

Thai Cabbage Salad | 131

Kale Salad | 133

Greek Spinach Salad | 134

Balsamic-Glazed Beet Salad with
Fennel & Arugula | 137

German Potato Salad | 138

Cucumber Raita Salad | 140

Curried Tofu Salad | 141

French Lentil & Couscous Salad | 142

Oriental Buckwheat Noodle Salad | 145

Sun-Dried Tomato Pesto Pasta Salad | 146

CURRIED CHICKEN SALAD

This is an excellent way to use up leftover chicken. The curry powder, cashew nuts, and apple give character to the somewhat bland meat.

Serves 4

- 2 chicken breasts
- 2 stalks finely chopped celery
- 1/3 cup finely chopped parsley
- 2 cups grated apples
- 3/4 cup roasted, chopped cashew nuts
- 2 tablespoons curry powder
- 1/2 cup mayonnaise
- 1/4 cup freshly squeezed orange juice
- 1 teaspoon cumin
- 1 teaspoon salt

Place the chicken breasts in a casserole dish and bake in a preheated oven at 350 degrees F for 30 minutes. Cool and cut into 1/2-inch cubes. Place the chicken in a mixing bowl and add the celery, parsley, apples, and nuts. Toss until blended.

Toast the curry powder in a dry skillet over medium-low heat until it has a strong, flavorful curry smell. Be sure to stir the curry powder as you toast it. Mix the mayonnaise, orange juice, cumin, salt and toasted curry together, and then add it to the chicken mixture and toss.

This salad can be served as a lunch for 4 people atop a bed of fresh salad greens or over 4 pieces of toasted whole-grain bread as open-faced sandwiches.

THAI CABBAGE SALAD

This is a perfect salad to accompany stir-fries or other oriental dishes such as Egg Foo Yong or Pad Thai. This recipe comes to Esalen by the grace of one of our Esalen office staff who worked as a tour guide in Thailand. The secret to a good cabbage salad is in the shredding. The shredding should be as thin as possible—paper-thin if you can. This releases more of the cabbage flavor and has an easier texture to chew.

Serves 4 to 6

 6 cups finely shredded green cabbage
 2 tablespoons rice wine vinegar
 2 tablespoons brown sugar
 3 tablespoons chopped cilantro
 1 teaspoon minced garlic
 1$^{1}/_{2}$ teaspoons sea salt
 $^{1}/_{4}$ cup dry-roasted peanuts
 1 cup sliced red bell pepper (sliced into thin $^{1}/_{2}$-inch strips)
 2 green onions (sliced in fine rounds)
 1 tablespoon roasted sesame oil

Be sure when you cut the cabbage that you remove the stem part and that you lay the flat side down and cut as thinly as possible. You want to have long, thin strips of cabbage.

Whisk together the vinegar, sesame oil, brown sugar, cilantro, garlic, and salt and place in a mixing bowl; add the cabbage, onions, and bell peppers and toss. Continue to toss while other dishes are being prepared for your meal to coat the salad as much as possible with the marinade. Drain off half the marinade just before serving. Chop peanuts and toss into salad last.

Kale Salad

KALE SALAD

Kale is the original plant that all the cabbage family evolved from. It is one of the most nutritious foods on the planet. Kale is an excellent source of vitamins, minerals, and enzymes. It is extremely rich in beta carotene, dietary fiber, and antioxidants. It is very low in fat and high in trace nutrients. The Esalen garden grows large crops of kale year-round, and we're glad they do because our staff and guests can't get enough of this salad.

Maggie Dawson, an extended student at Esalen, first started making kale salads in our kitchen. It didn't take long for this to become a standard dish on our salad bar.

Serves 4 to 6

- ⅓ cup Bragg Liquid Aminos or tamari soy sauce
- ⅓ cup lemon juice
- ⅓ cup flax seed oil or extra-virgin olive oil
- ½ medium-size red onion
- ¼ cup sunflower seeds
- ¼ cup pumpkin seeds
- ¼ cup sesame seeds
- 1 pound fresh kale
- ½ cup sunflower sprouts
- ½ cup alfalfa sprouts
- 1 avocado, cut into ½-inch cubes (optional)
- 1 cup thinly sliced shiitake or crimini mushrooms (optional)

K A L E

Red Russian and/or Siberian are nice choices, but any kale works as long as it's tender.

Combine the Bragg or soy sauce and lemon juice in a blender or whisk in a bowl. Slowly dribble in the oil as the blender turns or as you whisk vigorously. Slice the onion into thin half-moons and marinate in the dressing as you prepare the rest of the salad.

Toast the seeds in a heavy-bottomed pan (cast-iron is the best) over medium heat until seeds are just golden and fragrant. Toast each seed type separately as their size requires varying roasting times. Cool to room temperature.

Destem the kale; you can do this by holding the bottom of the kale stem in one hand and then running your other hand down the stem, pulling off all the leaves as your hand runs down the kale stem. Stack the kale leaves and slice into 1/4-inch ribbons. This is the most important step, so take your time. The success of this recipe lies in cutting the kale into small ribbons and in completely massaging the kale with the dressing.

Toss the seeds, sprouts, and kale together with the marinated onions and as much dressing as necessary to lightly but completely dress the kale. Massage the dressing into the kale with your hands. Add the avocado and mushrooms if using and toss again with your hands.

GREEK SPINACH SALAD

A regular summer lunch in the Esalen dining lodge is the Greek Feast. When the Esalen garden is full of fresh organic spinach, you will always find the Greek Feast on the menu. It includes hummus and pita bread alongside a large salad full of crisp spinach that has been picked just a few hours before serving, tossed with other vegetables and feta cheese. Our Greek Spinach Salad is dressed with a simple Lemon-Sage Vinaigrette.

Serves 4

6	cups small spinach leaves
1	cup sliced cucumber
1/4	cup extra-virgin olive oil
2	tablespoons freshly squeezed lemon juice
1	teaspoon minced garlic
1/4	teaspoon chopped fresh sage
1/4	teaspoon sea salt
	Pinch freshly ground white pepper
2	small red onions sliced in very fine rings
1	cup finely sliced crimini mushrooms
2	cups cherry tomatoes
1	cup pitted kalamata olives
1 1/2	cups crumbled feta cheese

Wash and stem the spinach; if the leaves are too large, rip into bite-size pieces. Peel the cucumbers and cut lengthwise down the middle; then scoop out the seeds with a spoon. Slice the cucumber halves into 1/4-inch slices, in the shape of horseshoes.

Whisk the oil, lemon juice, garlic, sage, salt, and pepper in the bottom of a large salad bowl until well blended. Add the cucumbers, onions, mushrooms, tomatoes, and olives. Toss these vegetables with the vinaigrette until they are well coated and then add the spinach and toss again. Finally, sprinkle the cheese into the salad and give it one final toss.

Balsamic-Glazed Beet Salad with
Fennel & Arugula

BALSAMIC-GLAZED BEET SALAD WITH FENNEL & ARUGULA

This is a real crowd-pleaser at the Esalen salad bar. The gardener brings into the kitchen baskets of freshly picked fennel and arugula that are added to the cooked beets. The reduction of the balsamic vinegar, the beets, and the fennel create a contrast with the sharp and piquant flavor of the arugula.

Serves 4 to 6

- 6 medium-size beets
- 3 bulbs fennel
- 5 cups chopped arugula*
- 1 cup balsamic vinegar
- 1/2 cup extra-virgin olive oil
-    Salt to taste

* If you can't find arugula, fresh spinach is a good replacement.

Place beets in a 4-quart saucepan and cover with water. Boil on high heat for approximately 1/2 hour; they are done when a knife goes into the beet without resistance. Place under cold running water to cool and peel off skin when cool enough to handle. Slice the beets into eighths and place in salad bowl.

Trim the fennel, cut in half, and slice into fine 1/4-inch slices. Place into bowl with beets. Chop the arugula into fine ribbons and add to the vegetables. Place the vinegar into a small saucepan over medium heat and reduce down to half (about 1/2 cup). Whisk the oil and salt into this reduction. Dribble over salad and toss well. Garnish with the feathery tips of the fennel tops.

HONEY-MUSTARD GLAZED TOFU

This recipe can be served with German Potato Salad to make a complete vegetarian meal. It's a great way to prepare tofu and can be used in many different vegetarian lunch and dinner menus.

1 pound firm tofu
4 tablespoons Dijon mustard
3 tablespoons honey
$^1/_2$ teaspoon salt
$1^1/_4$ cups warm vegetable stock or water

Drain the tofu and cut into 4 steaks. Place tofu steaks onto a clean kitchen towel and cover with another kitchen towel; then place a heavy weight on top of the tofu to press out as much water as possible. Let this press for about 20 minutes. The more water that is pressed out of the tofu, the more flavor it will absorb.

Whisk the mustard, honey, salt, and stock or water together until honey and salt are dissolved and all the ingredients are blended. Dip the tofu steaks into the mustard marinade and then place into an oiled baking dish.

Cover tofu with remaining marinade and place into an oven preheated to 350 degrees F. Bake uncovered for 30 minutes and then turn the steaks over and bake for another 30 minutes or until the marinade has been absorbed by the tofu. The steaks should have a brown, glazed appearance. Remove from oven and serve.

GERMAN POTATO SALAD

This is a light variation on the classic German dish. Served hot or warm, it has the possibility of accompanying many more dishes than the cold American-style potato salad. Unlike traditional German-style potato salad that is loaded with bacon and bacon fat, this recipe has the bacon flavor without the bacon or fat. We serve this salad along with bratwurst sausages or Honey-Mustard Glazed Tofu for a hearty midday meal.

Serves 4 as a lunch

2 pounds red potatoes, unpeeled
$^1/_4$ cup vegetable oil
2 tablespoons rice wine vinegar
$^1/_3$ cup minced red onion
2 teaspoons brown sugar
$1^1/_2$ teaspoons sea salt
$^1/_2$ teaspoon freshly ground black pepper
$^1/_2$ cup minced celery
2 tablespoons Baco Bits
2 green onions cut in fine rounds
1 tablespoon chopped fresh flat-leaf parsley
2 tablespoons chopped dill pickle
$^1/_2$ cup mayonnaise

Place the potatoes in a saucepan and cover with water. Bring to a boil on high heat, and then lower to a simmer for about 20 minutes or until done. The potatoes are ready when a knife goes into the potato easily but the potato is still firm. Don't overcook the potatoes or they will have a mushy texture. When they are done, pour off the water and let cool for 5 minutes.

While potatoes are cooling, place the oil, vinegar, onion, brown sugar, salt, and pepper in a saucepan and bring to a boil; then cut the heat. Slice potatoes into 3/4-inch cubes and place in a mixing bowl. Pour the hot vinegar marinade over warm potatoes and toss very gently once or twice. Let potatoes marinate for 5 minutes.

In another mixing bowl, blend the celery, Baco Bits, green onions, parsley, and pickle. Add this to potatoes and toss gently another two times. Add the mayonnaise and gently toss until mixed. Be careful: if you overmix, it turns out to be mashed potato salad.

CUCUMBER RAITA SALAD

Raita is the most common form of salad in India and makes a great accompaniment to hotter and spicier dishes. This salad is an accompaniment to the South Indian Coconut Curry that we serve at Esalen. The raita is a cooling accompaniment that imparts an added flavor to the hot-spicy curry and should be eaten alongside the curry. At Esalen, we mix up about seven gallons of this salad for an evening meal.

Serves 4

2	medium-size cucumbers
1	teaspoon cumin
1¹/₂	cups yogurt
1	cup sour cream
1	teaspoon salt
4	green onions, sliced in fine rounds

Peel cucumbers and cut in half lengthwise. Scoop out seeds with a spoon. Thinly slice cucumbers in a half-circle shape. Place the cumin in a dry frying pan and toast on medium heat until it has a pungent cumin smell. In a salad bowl, blend yogurt, sour cream, toasted cumin, and salt. Once this mixture is well blended, toss in the onions and cucumber slices. Serve with curries and other Indian dishes.

CURRIED TOFU SALAD

This is a great filling for sandwiches as well as a delightful high-protein vegetarian salad lunch. The crunchiness of the sunflower seeds and fresh vegetables and the spiciness of the curry makes this a light, tasty salad.

Serves 4

- 1 pound firm tofu
- $1/4$ cup sunflower seeds
- 2 tablespoons freshly squeezed lemon juice
- 1 teaspoon tamari soy sauce
- 2 tablespoons curry powder
- 1 tablespoon cumin powder
- $1^1/2$ teaspoons sea salt
- 2 teaspoons nutritional yeast
- 2 green onions, sliced into fine rounds
- $1/2$ cup grated carrots
- $1/2$ cup finely diced celery
- $1/2$ cup finely diced red bell pepper
- $1/2$ cup finely chopped kalamata olives
- $1/2$ cup minced flat-leaf parsley

Drain and press tofu of excess water. Rough chop it in a food processor or crumble by using a pastry cutter. Place the crumbled tofu in a mixing bowl and set aside. Roast sunflower seeds at 450 degrees F for 8 to 10 minutes. In a separate bowl, mix together the lemon juice, soy sauce, curry powder, cumin, salt, and nutritional yeast. Add this to the tofu and toss. Then add the onions, carrots, celery, peppers, olives, roasted sunflower seeds, and parsley to the bowl and toss until well blended. This salad can be served on a bed of lettuce or spinach. It can also be used as a sandwich filling.

FRENCH LENTIL & COUSCOUS SALAD

At one time in my life I lived and worked with a wine farmer in Provence, near the city of Avignon, France. After working all morning in the vineyards, the farmer's wife, Madame Ponsion, would bring lunch to us in the field. She was a great Provencal cook, and I learned many recipes from her. This is one that I loved and I brought along to Esalen, where it became a great lunch favorite.

Tina Wehr

Serves 4

1¹/₂ cups green french lentils
5 cups water
1 tablespoon thyme
1 tablespoon oregano
1 tablespoon basil
1 bay leaf
1 small branch fresh rosemary or 1 tablespoon rosemary
4 teaspoons salt, divided
1¹/₂ cups couscous
1 cup plus 1 tablespoon olive oil
2 medium Roma tomatoes, cored and chopped into small dice
1 carrot, finely diced
1 small red onion, finely diced
2 green onions, chopped in fine rounds
2 cups grated Asiago or Parmesan cheese
5 tablespoons finely chopped basil
1 tablespoon balsamic vinegar
1 clove garlic, minced
1 cup chopped arugula
1 cup chopped spinach

Check for stones in the lentils and remove. Rinse lentils well and cook in 5 cups water. Add the thyme, oregano, basil, bay leaf, rosemary branch, and 3 teaspoons of salt to the cooking water. Bring lentils up to a boil, and then reduce heat and let them simmer for about 20 minutes. Cook until the lentils are tender but firm. Don't overcook. Drain; take out the rosemary branch and bay leaf and discard, and then let cool.

Place couscous in mixing bowl and rub 1 tablespoon of olive oil into the couscous with your hands. Add enough boiling water to the couscous to just cover by about ⅛ inch. Seal immediately with a tight-fitting lid or plastic wrap and let sit to cool. After the couscous has reached room temperature, gently fluff it with a fork until it is light and not compact.

Lightly mix lentils with couscous. Add the tomatoes, carrot, onion, green onion, cheese, and fresh basil to the mix. Mix the 1 cup oil, the vinegar, garlic, and 1 teaspoon salt together and add this to the couscous-lentil mix; gently toss everything until well mixed. Cover the bottom of a platter with the arugula and spinach and then scoop the couscous-lentil salad over the greens. Serve at room temperature.

Oriental Buckwheat Noodle Salad

ORIENTAL BUCKWHEAT NOODLE SALAD

The robust, earthy flavor of the buckwheat (soba) noodles blends perfectly with the roasted sesame oil. If you use 100 percent buckwheat noodles, they have a very strong earthy flavor; if you prefer a less strong flavor, buy the noodles that have a blend of buckwheat and wheat flours. The ingredient list may seem a bit long for this salad, but it is easy to prepare and will keep for several days in the refrigerator.

Serves 4 to 6

- 1 tablespoon sea salt
- 1/2 pound dry buckwheat (soba) noodles
- 4 tablespoons toasted black or brown sesame seeds
- 1/2 cup roasted sesame oil
- 1/2 cup extra-virgin olive oil
- 5 teaspoons freshly squeezed lemon juice
- 1/2 cup fresh orange juice (from 1 large Valencia orange)
- 5 tablespoons tamari soy sauce
- 1/4 cup maple syrup
- 1/2 cup diced red bell pepper
- 2 cups sliced bok choy (sliced in fine ribbons and firmly packed)
- 1 small carrot, cut into matchsticks
- 1 cup snow peas, cut into 2-inch lengths
- 1 cup sliced button mushrooms
- 2 tablespoons minced fresh ginger
- 1 tablespoon minced garlic
- 2 tablespoons chopped fresh cilantro

Bring 2 quarts of water to a boil in a saucepan. Add 1 tablespoon sea salt to the water and slowly drop the noodles into the water as you stir. Cook the soba noodles for about 8 minutes or until the noodles are tender but not mushy. Take note that buckwheat noodles cook faster than semolina pasta. Place cooked noodles in a colander and rinse with cold water. Set aside and let drain.

Place the sesame seeds in a heavy-bottomed skillet and roast over high heat until they have a sweet, toasty smell. In a small mixing bowl, add the oils, lemon juice, and orange juice. Whisk until blended, and then whisk in the soy sauce and maple syrup.

Place noodles in a bowl, add the sauce, and toss; then add the vegetables, mushrooms, toasted sesame seeds, ginger, garlic, and cilantro. Toss well and serve or refrigerate for later.

SUN-DRIED
TOMATO PESTO

1/2 cup sun-dried tomatoes

1/4 cup warm water

2 cloves garlic

1 cup fresh basil, stemmed and
  roughly chopped

1/4 cup fresh oregano, stemmed and
  roughly chopped

1/2 cup extra-virgin olive oil

1/4 teaspoon ground black pepper

1 teaspoon sea salt

Soak the tomatoes in the water for
10 minutes or until tomatoes become soft.
Place tomatoes with the soaking water
into a blender or food processor with a
chopping attachment. Add the garlic, basil,
oregano, olive oil, pepper, and salt; blend
until you have a thick paste.

SUN-DRIED TOMATO PESTO PASTA SALAD

This pasta salad can be served cold as a summer lunch or warm accompanying a main dish. If you use sun-dried tomatoes that are packed in olive oil, you can use the oil for making the pesto which will give it added flavor.

Serves 4 to 6

1 medium-size red onion, cut in 1/2-inch dice

2 medium-size zucchini, cut in 1/2-inch dice

1 eggplant, cut in 1/2-inch dice

2 tablespoons olive oil

1 teaspoon salt

3/4 cup pine nuts

2 cups dry orecchiette, shell, or penne pasta

1 recipe Sun-Dried Tomato Pesto

1 cup roughly chopped arugula

1 cup grated Parmesan or Asiago cheese

Toss the fresh vegetables in a mixing bowl with the olive oil and salt. Place on a baking sheet and in an oven preheated to 450 degrees F and bake until they are slightly brown and have a shriveled look, about 30 minutes. Set aside to cool.

In a heavy-bottomed skillet, pan-roast the pine nuts over medium heat. Be sure to flip or stir the nuts as they roast.

In a 2-quart saucepan over high heat, bring 1 1/2 quarts of water with 1 tablespoon of salt to a boil. Stir in the pasta. When the mixture comes to a boil, lower heat to a simmer and cook for about 11 minutes. Remove from heat and strain in a colander. Place the pasta in a large mixing bowl with the Sun-Dried Tomato Pesto. Add the roasted veggies, pine nuts, arugula, and cheese to the pasta and toss.

DRESSINGS

Orange-Basil Vinaigrette | 148

Apple-Dijon Salad Dressing | 148

Ginger-Miso Salad Dressing | 149

Eggless Caesar Salad Dressing | 149

Shirley's Mix Salad Dressing | 150

Spiral Salad Dressing | 150

Lite Asian Salad Dressing | 151

Angel Dream Salad Dressing | 152

Enlightened Balsamic Salad Dressing | 153

ORANGE-BASIL VINAIGRETTE

This dressing enjoys a regular rotation on our salad bar in part because it is so easy to make. Although orange juice concentrate and fresh basil are not the most glamorous ingredients, they do help this dressing complement a bowl of greens.

Makes 1 3/4 cups

- 3/4 cup olive oil
- 2 tablespoons apple cider vinegar
- 2 tablespoons rice wine vinegar
- 5 tablespoons frozen orange juice concentrate, thawed
- 2 tablespoons minced fresh basil
- 1/4 teaspoon salt

Mix all ingredients in a blender or with a whisk, or shake in a jar with a tight-fitting lid. This dressing will keep for several days if kept in a sealed container and stored in the fridge.

APPLE-DIJON SALAD DRESSING

This spinach-friendly dressing is great on other vegetables as well as salads. Try it with steamed green beans, Brussels sprouts, or kale. At Esalen, we used a sugar-free apple butter to make this recipe.

Makes 1 1/2 cups

- 3/4 cup extra-virgin olive oil
- 1/3 cup apple butter
- 1 tablespoon Dijon mustard
- 1/4 cup freshly squeezed lemon juice
- 1 tablespoon red or brown rice miso paste
- 1 teaspoon minced garlic
- 1/4 teaspoon sea salt

Place all the ingredients into a blender and blend for 2 minutes until mixed well. (If you don't have a blender, whisk all ingredients together in a mixing bowl until smooth.) This dressing keeps for several days if kept in a sealed container and stored in the fridge.

GINGER-MISO SALAD DRESSING

Silken tofu is a silky textured tofu that works great to thicken salad dressings, giving them a very creamy texture. In this recipe, it blends in with fresh ginger and red miso to create a creamy Asian dressing.

Makes about 1$^1/_2$ cups

- 1 block silken tofu
- 2 tablespoons rice wine vinegar
- Juice of 1 orange
- 2 tablespoons minced fresh ginger
- 2 tablespoons red miso soybean paste
- 1 tablespoon chopped fresh basil
- $^1/_4$ teaspoon salt

Mix all ingredients in a blender or whisk by hand. Keeps for several days in the fridge.

EGGLESS CAESAR SALAD DRESSING

For those of you who love a good Caesar salad but don't enjoy the thought of eating raw egg, then you have found your savior. Actually, this is a great creamy dressing for lots of salads, including your favorite Caesar.

Makes about 2 cups

- $^1/_2$ avocado
- $^1/_3$ cup freshly squeezed lemon juice
- $^1/_4$ cup rice wine vinegar
- 1 cup olive oil
- $^1/_2$ teaspoon salt
- 2 fillets anchovies (optional)
- 1 tablespoon minced garlic

Put avocado, lemon juice, and vinegar in a blender and blend until you have a smooth paste. Add olive oil and blend until you have a creamy texture. Then add salt, garlic, and anchovies if using and blend until smooth and creamy. This dressing keeps for up to 2 days, covered, in the fridge.

SHIRLEY'S MIX SALAD DRESSING

This is a simple light dressing that serves as a complement to a salad mix without covering up the delicate flavor of the fresh greens. It's an excellent dressing for bitter lettuces and greens.

Makes about 1 cup

- 1/2 cup olive oil
- 3 tablespoons balsamic vinegar
- 2 tablespoons tamari
- 2 tablespoons maple syrup
- 1 clove garlic, minced

Mix all ingredients in blender or with a whisk. This dressing keeps for several days if sealed and stored in the fridge.

SPIRAL SALAD DRESSING

When I was in charge of the Esalen kitchen, this was by far the most requested recipe from diners. It's an Asian-flavored salad dressing that blends sweet, sour, and salty. We have a steady production of Spiral Salad Dressing in the kitchen, mixing it up in 5-gallon batches. It's also tasty served over steamed broccoli or chard.

Makes 2 cups

- 1/2 cup olive oil
- 2 tablespoons red wine vinegar
- 2 tablespoons rice wine vinegar
- 2 tablespoons tamari soy sauce
- 2 tablespoons honey
- 1 1/2 tablespoons mellow or white miso soybean paste
- 1/4 cup grated fresh ginger
- 2 tablespoons water
- 1 medium red onion, minced

Mix all ingredients in blender or whisk by hand. Will hold in the refrigerator for 1 week.

LITE ASIAN SALAD DRESSING

This is Esalen's lowest calorie salad dressing. It has almost no oil. It was developed by Jason Brodsky, an extended student who was determined to satisfy the diets of our calorie-counting guests. It soon became one of Esalen's favorites.

Makes 1 cup

- ¼ cup rice wine vinegar
- ¼ cup tamari soy sauce
- 2 tablespoons honey
- 2 scallions, minced
- 1 teaspoon minced garlic
- 1 teaspoon roasted sesame oil
- 1 teaspoon grated fresh ginger
- ½ teaspoon lemon juice

Place all ingredients in blender or whisk by hand. Add water to get the desired consistency. This dressing will keep for several days in the fridge.

ANGEL DREAM SALAD DRESSING

One of the Esalen chefs, Angela Karegeannes, created this recipe. She told me this story: "This dressing was created on a rainy day in the Upper East Side of Manhattan on the corner of 70th and 2nd streets with only the ingredients I could find in my boyfriend's fridge. I brought it to Esalen and expanded it with my dear friend Maggie, who quickly became a huge fan of it. This dressing has a sneaky way of making a salad feel like a meal without being a heavy dressing. The combination of tahini, tamari, lime juice, and mint seems to evoke the essence of the Greece, Japan, Thailand, and the California coast all at the same time. The tarragon makes for an unexpectedly delicious complement."

Makes 1 1/2 cups

- 1/2 cup water
- 2 tablespoons tamari
- 1 tablespoon maple syrup
- 2 tablespoons freshly squeezed lemon juice
- 1/4 cup sesame tahini
- 2 teaspoons finely chopped fresh tarragon
- 2 teaspoons finely chopped fresh dill leaf
- 2 teaspoons finely chopped fresh mint

Place everything into a blender and mix for 2 minutes until smooth.

If you don't have a blender, follow these directions: In a bowl, mix the water, tamari, maple syrup, and lemon juice. Add the tahini and whisk until smooth. Whisk in the fresh herbs and enjoy!

This dressing will keep for several days if sealed and stored in the fridge.

ENLIGHTENED BALSAMIC SALAD DRESSING

Building your own salad at Esalen is quite a treat, especially in the summer when the salad bar overflows with an abundance of crisp vegetables and lettuces that have been freshly picked and washed just hours before by the Esalen gardeners. Our homemade salad dressings are a great complement to this abundance. This recipe is a sweet variation on the traditional balsamic vinaigrette.

Makes about 1¾ cups

- ¾ cup olive oil
- ¾ cup balsamic vinegar
- 1 tablespoon Dijon mustard
- 2 teaspoons honey
- Juice of 1 lemon
- Juice of 1 orange
- 2 teaspoons maple syrup
- 2 teaspoons dry basil
- ¼ teaspoon salt
- Pinch cayenne pepper

Mix all ingredients in a blender or with a whisk, or shake in a jar with a tight-fitting lid. This dressing keeps for several days in the fridge.

SOUPS

Fresh Tomato Soup | 156

Cream of Tomato Soup | 158

Roasted Carrot Soup | 159

Roasted Butternut & Curry Soup | 160

Vegetarian French Onion Soup | 162

Ginger Yam Soup | 163

Fresh Corn Chowder | 164

Clam Chowder | 165

Hearty Minestrone Soup | 166

Chilled Gazpacho Soup | 169

Ayurvedic Dal | 170

FRESH TOMATO SOUP

This soup has the really fresh taste of summer. It's a great recipe to make when tomato season has reached its peak and tomatoes are most flavorful. Try different varieties of tomatoes to bring out different flavors.

Serves 4

2 tablespoons butter
1 medium-size red onion, cut in $1/4$-inch dice
4 cups diced fresh tomatoes, cut in $1/2$-inch dice
1 teaspoon minced garlic
2 cups vegetable stock or water
1 teaspoon paprika
1 tablespoon maple syrup
2 teaspoons sea salt
$1/2$ teaspoon cayenne pepper
2 tablespoons freshly chopped dill

In a 6-quart soup pot over medium heat, melt the butter and sauté the onion until transparent. Add the tomatoes and garlic and cook 3 minutes more. Add vegetable stock or water, paprika, syrup, salt, and cayenne and bring to a boil.

Lower the heat and simmer for 10 minutes. Smooth the texture of the soup by placing it, in batches, in a blender or food processor. Or you can use a hand immersion blender. Return the pureed soup to the pot over low heat. Bring up to serving temperature, but don't let the soup boil. Garnish with fresh dill before serving.

VEGAN VERSION

To make this into a vegan soup, replace the butter with olive oil.

CREAM OF TOMATO SOUP

This is one of the Esalen staff favorites, brought to us by Bill Herr. I suspect many people's flavor image of tomato soup is heavily influenced by an early overexposure to Campbell's Tomato Soup. This version of Cream of Tomato Soup (made with milk), while not a slavish imitation, does pay homage to the nostalgia.

Serves 4

- 1 tablespoon finely diced onion
- 4 tablespoons unsalted butter
- 5 tablespoons unbleached all-purpose flour
- 3 cups milk
- 4 cups tomato juice
  Sea salt and pepper to taste

Briefly sauté onion in butter over medium heat until translucent. Whisk in flour to make a roux. Add milk, a cup at a time, mixing well and allowing mixture to thicken after each addition. Stir in tomato juice, season with salt and pepper, and heat to serving temperature.

Jason Brodsky

VEGAN VERSION

Replace milk with soy milk, and butter with a good quality vegetable margarine.

ROASTED CARROT SOUP

Jason Brodsky, a professional sound engineer for rock music groups, decided to take a year off and explore his inner self at Esalen. He created this recipe in the Esalen kitchen while living and working in our community. He turned out to be a very creative cook, and since he was a vegan, he added a number of vegan recipes to our kitchen. He is now back traveling around the world working with musicians. He asked me to tell you that you must prepare this soup while listening to good music—it gives it a better taste!

Serves 4 to 6

     5   pounds carrots
     1   medium-size apple
     2   tablespoons olive oil
     1   teaspoon sea salt
     1   teaspoon ground white pepper
     1   tablespoon vegetable oil
    3/4 cup diced white onion (cut in 1/2-inch dice)
     2   teaspoons minced garlic
     8   cups vegetable stock or water
     1   teaspoon apple cider vinegar
         Salt to taste

Preheat oven to 350 degrees F. Cut the carrots and apple into thirds and toss them in a mixing bowl with the olive oil, salt, and pepper. Once they are coated with the oil mixture, place them on a baking sheet and roast in the oven until slightly brown, about 45 minutes.

In a 6-quart soup pot over medium heat, sauté onion in vegetable oil until it becomes translucent, and then add garlic and sauté for 1 minute more. Add the vegetable stock or water, and then turn up the heat to high and bring to a boil. Lower the heat to simmer and drop in the baked carrots and apple.

It's necessary to puree this soup. This can be done easily by using an immersion blender (also called a hand or stick blender). Or you can pour the soup into a blender in 3 or 4 batches and puree it. If you have none of the above available, the last resort is to use a potato masher and mash the vegetables as best as possible; finish with a whisk.

Return the pureed soup to pot and let it simmer for about 2 hours. It may be necessary to skim the top of the soup during the simmering if a natural foam-like substance appears. Finish the soup by adding the vinegar and salting to taste before serving.

ROASTED BUTTERNUT & CURRY SOUP

Most people have eaten butternut squash without knowing it. The canned pumpkin that is found in the supermarket that a lot of people make pumpkin pie out of is, in all honesty, butternut squash. Butternut has an exceptionally good flavor and a creamy texture. Roasting concentrates the sugars and flavor of this orange-fleshed winter squash. The spicy curry and the creaminess of the coconut milk give this soup another dynamic.

Serves 4 to 6

- 1 large butternut squash
- 2 tablespoons vegetable oil
- 1 medium-size onion, cut into ¼-inch dice
- 2 stalks celery, cut into ¼-inch dice
- 2 tablespoons curry powder
- 3 cups coconut milk
- 2 teaspoons sea salt
- 3 cups chicken stock, vegetable stock, or water
- 1 tablespoon chopped cilantro
  Sunflower seeds for garnish (optional)

Place a large butternut on a baking tray and bake in a preheated oven at 400 degrees F. Roast for about 1 hour; it is done when you can stick a knife into the squash and there is no resistance (it goes through like butter). Split the squash in half; scoop out and discard the seeds. Scoop out the pulp and set aside.

Place oil in a 6-quart soup pot over high heat and sauté onion until it is translucent, about 5 minutes. Then add the celery and curry powder and sauté until the celery is tender. Turn heat down to medium and add the butternut pulp, coconut milk, salt, and stock or water. Blend with a hand mixer or whisk by hand until you have a smooth consistency. Heat until soup is hot, add cilantro, and serve.

VARIATION

For an excellent taste, add chunks of fresh goat cheese or fresh cream to the soup before serving.

VEGETARIAN FRENCH ONION SOUP

At the Esalen kitchen, students from the Culinary Institute of America come and fill their internship requirements for their degree. This French onion soup recipe was created by Talia Rotter, one of the culinary students who, after her graduation, came back to Esalen to work as a staff chef. Red onions, tomato paste, and soy sauce give this soup that real full-body brown flavor without using meat stock.

Serves 6

- 1 head garlic
  Olive oil
- 6 large red onions
- 2 tablespoons vegetable oil
- 2 tablespoons tomato paste
- 8 cups vegetable stock or water
- 1 teaspoon freshly chopped rosemary
- 1/2 cup tamari soy sauce

Cut the top off the garlic head and drizzle with a drop of olive oil. Place in an oven preheated to 450 degrees F and roast until the cloves are soft and it starts to have a sweet aroma.

Peel and chop the onions; first in half, then in half again, and then slice into 1/4-inch quarter moons. Place a small amount of vegetable oil into a heavy-bottomed 4-quart soup pot and sauté the onions over medium-high heat until they turn translucent. Lower the heat and slowly cook onions until they start to be a caramelized golden brown, about 30 more minutes.

Add the tomato paste and continue to sauté for a couple minutes more. Take the garlic head out of the oven and squeeze the pulp out of each clove. Place the roasted garlic pulp into the soup pot and add the stock or water. Add rosemary and soy sauce and bring the soup to a boil. Lower the heat to a simmer, cover, and cook for 45 minutes. Serve with herb croutons.

HERB CROUTONS

- 4 slices old, dry bread (Sourdough Rye is my favorite, see page 38)
- 3 tablespoons olive oil
- 1/4 teaspoon dry basil
- 1/4 teaspoon dry oregano
- 1/4 teaspoon paprika
  Pinch salt

Sourdough rye bread is my favorite to use for making croutons. In a medium bowl, mix the herbs, paprika, and salt with the oil. Cut the crust off the bread and cut bread into 1/2-inch cubes. Toss the bread cubes in the oil mixture until they absorb all the oil. Spread out on a baking sheet and bake in a preheated oven at 375 degrees F for 10 to 15 minutes or until crisp. Turn the croutons halfway through baking. Baking time will vary depending on the age and dryness of the bread. Croutons can be used immediately or stored in a sealed container.

GINGER YAM SOUP

Balancing the warming, spicy flavor of the ginger with the sweetness of the yams is what makes this simple-to-prepare soup a tasty success. Fresh ginger not only adds great flavor to food, but it also acts as a tonic for the whole body, especially the lungs and sinuses.

Serves 4

- 2 tablespoons olive oil
- 1 medium-size yellow onion, cut into $1/2$-inch dice
- $1^1/_2$ pounds of garnet yams, peeled and cut into 1-inch dice
- $1^1/_2$ teaspoons ground cumin
- 2 teaspoons salt
- 1 tablespoon grated fresh ginger
- 5 cups water
- 2 tablespoons chopped scallions

Melt the butter in a saucepan over medium heat, add the onion, and sauté for about 10 minutes or until golden brown. Add the yams to the onions, sauté for 3 minutes more, and then add the cumin, salt, ginger, and water.

Lower the heat, cover, and let simmer for about 30 minutes.

Place mixture into a blender in batches, or use an immersion blender, and puree until smooth. Return to the soup pot if needed and warm through. If a thinner consistency is desired, add water. If a richer taste is desired, add a little cream. Sprinkle the scallions over the top and serve.

FRESH CORN CHOWDER

From the beginning, whenever the Esalen kitchen served meat or fish, it always provided an alternative for vegetarians. Currently, approximately 25 percent of the Esalen staff and guests are vegetarians. In the early days, before vegetarian cuisine was common, the alternative vegetarian protein would be a chunk of cheese. The kitchen has evolved since those days and now serves a world-class vegetarian fare. Here is a recipe created by Robin Burnside that is often served as an alternative to Clam Chowder.

Serves 4 to 6

2	tablespoons olive oil
1	large onion, cut into $1/2$-inch dice
2	stalks celery, cut into $1/4$-inch dice
$2^{1}/2$	cups freshly cut corn or frozen corn
2	cups diced red potatoes
$1/3$	cup diced red bell pepper
3	cups vegetable stock or water
1	tablespoon minced garlic
2	fresh bay leaves
1	cup half-and-half, scalded
1	teaspoon nutmeg
$1/4$	cup fresh parsley
$2^{1}/2$	teaspoons sea salt
$1/2$	teaspoon white pepper

Pour the oil in a 6-quart soup pot over medium heat and sauté the onion until it begins to brown. Add celery, corn, potatoes, and bell pepper and sauté for 5 minutes more. Then add the vegetable stock or water, garlic, and bay leaves. Cover and lower the heat to simmer. Let this cook for about 20 to 30 minutes or until the potatoes are done but still firm.

Pour 1 cup of the soup in a blender and blend until smooth, and then return it to the soup pot. This will help give the chowder a creamy texture. Add the half-and-half, nutmeg, parsley, salt, and pepper. Warm through.

CLAM CHOWDER

Chowder Feast is a once-a-month menu item at Esalen, especially during the colder months. Our famous fish cook, John Blunt, would always be on hand to cook up his three types of tasty chowders. Here is his recipe for the New England version.

Serves 4

- 5 tablespoons unsalted butter
- 1 medium-size yellow onion, cut into ¼-inch dice
- ¾ cups unbleached all-purpose flour
- 1 (16-ounce) can clam juice
- 1 pound chopped clams, drained
- 1 pound red potatoes, cut into ½-inch dice
- 1 stalk celery, cut into ¼-inch dice
- 1 teaspoon sea salt
  Pinch ground white pepper
- 1 cup half-and-half
- 1 tablespoon freshly chopped flat-leaf parsley
- 1 tablespoon freshly chopped basil
- 1 tablespoon freshly chopped thyme

In a 6-quart soup pot, melt the butter and sauté the onion for 5 minutes or until it becomes translucent. Stir in the flour until it is well mixed with the onion and then add the clam juice. Bring this all to a boil, and then add the clams, potatoes, celery, salt, pepper, and half-and-half. Bring back to a boil, and then lower the heat to a simmer. Let the chowder slowly simmer uncovered for 30 minutes. Remove from heat and add the parsley, basil, and thyme.

HEARTY MINESTRONE SOUP

This is a fragrant and hearty soup that is perfect for a cold winter day. It can serve as the center of a meal or as a first course to a light meal.

Serves 6 to 8

- 1/2 pound uncooked small white beans or cannellini beans
- 1 tablespoon dry sage
- 1 tablespoon dry thyme
- 1 tablespoon dry rosemary
- 1 tablespoon dry savory
- 2 teaspoons sea salt
- 2 medium-size red onions, cut into 1/2-inch dice
- 2 tablespoons vegetable oil
- 1 tablespoon minced garlic
- 3 medium-size carrots, cut into 1/2-inch dice
- 2 medium-size zucchini, cut into 1/2-inch dice
- 1 cup red cooking wine
- 1 pound Roma tomatoes, cut into 1/2-inch dice
- 3 cups water
- 1 cup reserved white bean stock
- 1 cup cooked small pasta (cooked al dente)
- 4 large Swiss chard leaves, chopped into 1/4-inch ribbons

Sort the dry beans and discard any rocks, dirt clumps, or broken beans. Place beans in a 4-quart saucepan with 4 cups of water. Bring to a boil and then take off the heat and let sit for 1 hour. Pour beans into a colander and rinse well. Return the beans to the pot and add fresh water, sage, thyme, rosemary, savory, and salt. Cook beans until tender, about 1 hour. Drain and save stock.

Sauté the onion in the vegetable oil over high heat until it turns translucent. Add the garlic and sauté for 1 minute more, and then add the carrots and zucchini, sautéing for 2 minutes more. Add the wine and lower the heat to a simmer; let the mixture simmer for a few minutes. Add the tomatoes, water, and reserved bean stock. Turn up the heat to high, bring to a boil, and then reduce heat to a simmer. Cover and let the soup simmer for 15 minutes. Add the beans, pasta, and chard to the soup and let it simmer for another 10 minutes. Add salt to taste if needed.

Chilled Gazpacho Soup

CHILLED GAZPACHO SOUP

This chunky, ice-cold, uncooked soup recipe came from Barcelona, Spain. I taught natural-food cooking in this Mediterranean city, and on one of those visits I was a houseguest of a natural-food store owner. She prepared this raw soup for me one afternoon, and I was hooked. I had it every lunch during my stay.

Serves 4

    2   pounds Roma tomatoes
    1   medium-size cucumber, peeled
    2   tablespoons extra-virgin olive oil
    1   medium-size green bell pepper
    2   stalks celery
  3/4   cup pitted, dry-cured olives
    1   clove garlic, minced
    1   tablespoon chopped fresh basil
  1/4   teaspoon cayenne pepper
    2   tablespoons chopped fresh cilantro
 1 1/2   teaspoons sea salt
    2   teaspoons ground cumin

Core the tomatoes. Place three-fourths of the tomatoes, half of the cucumber, and the olive oil in a blender and liquefy. Chop the remainder of the tomatoes and cucumber, along with the bell pepper and celery, into very fine dice. Chop olives in small rounds. Add all chopped vegetables to the liquefied tomatoes and cucumber. Stir in the garlic, basil, cayenne, cilantro, and salt. Heat the cumin in a dry frying pan until its bouquet of flavor opens up. Stir this into the soup and chill in the fridge for at least 2 hours. Serve cold.

CHANNA DAL OR MASOOR DAL

In India, *dal* literally means dried split lentils and split peas. Split peas and lentils are much faster cooking than the whole legume, and this is one of the main reasons Indian cooks use them. *Channa dal* is split baby chickpeas, and *masoor dal* is a salmon-colored split pea that is also known as red split lentils. Dal is often served over rice in India and as a soup.

AYURVEDIC DAL

Ayurvedic is a five-thousand-year-old science of medicine that originated in India. The Ayurvedic healing method acknowledges the importance of food in healing the body. One of our chefs, Liam McDermott, took an Ayurvedic cooking course at Esalen. He brought this very well-balanced soup recipe into our kitchen, sometimes serving it as a hearty breakfast.

Serves 4 to 6

- 2 cups channa dal or masoor dal
- 8 cups water
- 1 medium carrot, cut into $1/2$-inch dice
- 2 tablespoons peeled and minced fresh ginger, divided
- 2 tablespoons curry powder
- 2 tablespoons vegetable oil or ghee
- 5 green onions, thinly sliced
- 1 cup raisins
- $1/4$ cup tomato paste
- 1 can (14 ounces) coconut milk
- 2 teaspoons sea salt
- 1 tablespoon chopped fresh cilantro

Rinse the dal, or lentils, under running water until the milky colored water runs clear. The dal may lump, and you may have to break it apart with your fingers as the water is washing it. Place dal into a 4-quart saucepan with water and bring to a boil. Reduce heat to simmer and add the carrot and 1 teaspoon of the ginger. Cover and let this simmer for 1/2 hour or until dal is soft.

Continued on page 172

In a small, dry skillet over low heat, toast the curry powder until it has a strong, fragrant smell of curry. Set aside. Put oil in a sauté pan over medium heat. When the pan is hot, add the green onions, remaining ginger, and raisins. Sauté for 2 minutes, and then add the tomato paste and sauté for 2 minutes more.

Add the toasted curry powder to the sauté pan, mix well, and then add this to the cooking dal along with the coconut milk and salt. Simmer for 20 minutes, uncovered, over low heat. The consistency of the dal should be fairly thick; it's almost a paste-like soup. It should not be made thinner. Take off heat and stir in the fresh cilantro. This soup will keep for 3 to 4 days in the fridge and will be as tasty as fresh-made.

SAUCES, SALSAS, AND SPREADS

HEALTHY HOISIN SAUCE

This recipe is a far cry better than the canned variety of hoisin sauce that is found in oriental shops and supermarkets. This sweet, sour, and spicy sauce can be used in stir-fries or as a marinade for meats, tofu, and tempeh.

Makes 1/2 cup

- 5 tablespoons red miso (soybean paste)
- 3 tablespoons dehydrated cane juice or brown sugar
- 3 tablespoons apple cider vinegar
- 1/4 teaspoon cayenne pepper
- 1/4 teaspoon ground fennel
- 1/2 teaspoon chopped fresh garlic
- 1/2 teaspoon chopped fresh ginger
  Pinch ground cloves
- 1/2 teaspoon roasted sesame oil
- 2 tablespoons frozen apple juice concentrate, thawed

Dissolve the miso, cane juice, and vinegar in a blender. Add all other ingredients and blend until smooth. This sauce will retain its quality over several days when kept in a sealed container in the fridge.

CHIPOTLE CREAM SAUCE

This spicy cream sauce is a complement to any Mexican meal. We've used it alongside our Griddle Corn Cakes and Crab Cakes at Esalen. It uses canned chipotle peppers in adobo sauce that are found in the Mexican food section of most supermarkets.

- 2 teaspoons chipotle peppers in adobo sauce
- 1 cup sour cream
- 1 tablespoon half-and-half
  Pinch sea salt

Place all ingredients in a blender and blend until smooth. If a blender isn't available, mash the peppers with a fork, then add the other ingredients and whisk until smooth.

TERIYAKI SAUCE

This is a classic Japanese sweet-and-salty sauce. It's an excellent marinade for baked chicken or tofu and is great in stir-fries. Use it as a sauce the Egg Foo Yong recipe (see page 65).

Makes 3 cups

- 1 cup tamari soy sauce
- 1 tablespoon roasted sesame oil
- 2 cups Mirin rice cooking wine
- $^1/_2$ cup honey
- $^1/_2$ cup warm water
- 1 clove garlic, minced
- $^1/_2$ teaspoon cayenne pepper
- $^1/_2$ teaspoon ground black mustard seed
- $^1/_2$ teaspoon wasabi radish powder

In a blender or with a whisk, blend the soy sauce, oil, wine, honey, and water. Add the garlic, cayenne, mustard seed, and wasabi. Blend well.

TERIYAKI GLAZE

We use this sauce in the Esalen kitchen to finish off many stir-fries. Simply add $^1/_4$ cup of arrowroot to the other ingredients for the Teriyaki Sauce and blend. It thickens as soon as it touches the heat and coats the stir-fry with a nice teriyaki glaze.

GREEN OLIVE & ROASTED ROMA TOMATO SAUCE

This is an old family recipe that was passed down from my Sicilian grandmother. It has the sharpness of green olives that contrast with the concentrated flavor of the roasted tomatoes. The addition of dried apricots and fennel seed helps to offset the acidity of the tomatoes. The only change I made to Grandma's recipe was substituting maple syrup for the refined sugar that is used if the sauce still has a strong acid taste. This is a very versatile sauce that can be used with many Italian and Provencal dishes.

Makes 6 cups

   3   pounds Roma tomatoes
   1   small yellow onion, cut into $\frac{1}{2}$-inch dice
       Olive oil
   1   tablespoon minced garlic
   2   cups canned tomato sauce
   $\frac{1}{2}$ teaspoon fennel seed
   $\frac{1}{2}$ teaspoon dried basil
   $\frac{1}{2}$ teaspoon dried oregano
   4   dried apricots, minced
   $\frac{1}{2}$ teaspoon salt
   2   cups pitted green olives, coarsely chopped
   1   tablespoon fresh basil
   1   tablespoon maple syrup (optional)

Preheat oven to 375 degrees F. Pare out the stem end of the tomatoes. Arrange them on a lightly oiled baking sheet and bake for about 30 minutes or until their skins start to crack and the tomatoes have a wilted, slightly dried appearance. Remove from oven and let cool. When cool, cut in half and scoop out the seeds and discard.

In a 4-quart saucepan over high heat, sauté the onion in a small amount of olive oil until it becomes translucent. (Do not use an aluminum saucepan to make this sauce.) Add the garlic and cook for 2 minutes more. Add the tomato sauce, fennel, dried basil, oregano, apricots, and salt. Bring this to a boil, and then reduce to a simmer. Add the roasted tomatoes and puree the sauce. (You can use an immersion blender, food processor, or even a potato masher for this.)

Add the olives. (If your olives came in salty brine, rinse them in hot tap water and drain before adding them to the sauce.) Continue to simmer and reduce the sauce until it is thick enough to coat the back of a wooden spoon, yet still thin enough to pour. Remove from heat and stir in the fresh basil. If the sauce has an acidic taste, add the maple syrup.

Serve over Torino Hazelnut Polenta (see page 91) or Aubergine Niçoise (see page 110).

ALUMINUM AND HIGH-ACID FOODS

If you're using an aluminum baking sheet for roasting the tomatoes, cover the pan with parchment paper first. Never cook highly acidic foods using aluminum pans. Their acidity will dissolve the soft metal that will then contaminate the food.

PORCINI MUSHROOM SAUCE

In Italian, the word porcine *means "little pigs." Porcine or King Boletus mushrooms are called the king of mushrooms. Porcinis are by far the most sought-after edible wild mushroom. Even dried, their smell and flavor are exceptional. Porcini mushrooms have an earthy, nutty flavor with a very meaty texture. This is a tasteful sauce that can be used on many dishes, including Spinach-Potato Roulade (see page 112).*

Makes 4 cups

- 1 cup dry porcini mushrooms
- 1^1/$_2$ cups vegetable stock or warm water
- ^{1}/$_4$ cup butter
- ^{1}/$_4$ cup unbleached all-purpose flour
- 1 cup half-and-half
- 1 teaspoon sea salt
- Pinch white pepper
- 1 tablespoon chopped fresh parsley

Rinse the mushrooms in a strainer, and then soak them in 1 cup warm stock or water for about 5 minutes or until the mushrooms are soft and pliable.

Over low heat, melt butter in a 1-quart saucepan, and then whisk in flour until smooth. Stir in the mushrooms with the soaking liquid and raise the heat to medium; stir often until this mixture boils.

Add the half-and-half, salt, and pepper. Keep the heat at medium and stir constantly until the mixture boils. Add the parsley and turn off the heat. The sauce is ready to serve.

VEGAN VERSION

To make a vegan version of the Porcini Mushroom Sauce, substitute the ^{1}/$_4$ cup butter with 1/4 cup unhydrogenated margarine, and substitute the 1 cup half-and-half with 1 cup soy milk.

TOMATILLO SALSA

This Mexican green sauce can be substituted for tomato salsas and makes a nice change from the expected.

Makes 6 cups

- 16 tomatillos (golf-ball size)
- 3 jalapeno or serrano chiles
- 2 medium-size yellow onions, cut into 1/4-inch dice
- 1 clove garlic, minced
- 2 teaspoons salt
  Juice of 6 limes
- 2 tablespoons chopped fresh cilantro
- 1 avocado, peeled, pitted, and cut into 1/4-inch dice

Peel and rinse the tomatillos. Chop them into 1/4-inch cubes and place in a mixing bowl. Pierce the chiles with a fork and roast them over an open flame (or place on a baking sheet and roast in the oven at 400 degrees F). Sear chiles until the skin turns black, then put them in a brown paper bag until they cool. When cool enough to handle, remove stem, skin, and seeds from the chiles and discard; finely mince chiles and add to the tomatillos. Be careful to wear gloves or wash your hands thoroughly after handling the chiles.

Add the onions and garlic to the tomatillos and chiles. Add the salt, lime juice, and cilantro. Gently mix the salsa until blended. Take one-third of the salsa and puree in a blender. Pour the puree back into the mixing bowl, add the avocado, and gently mix.

CASHEW CHEESE

This is a spread that we use at Esalen for our dairy-free cheese replacement. It can be used as sandwich filling, on pizza, or as a dip for chips and crudités.

Make 3 cups

- 1 cup cashew pieces
- 1/2 cup tahini
- 1/4 cup water
- 2 teaspoons tamari soy sauce
- 1/2 cup diced red pimentos, drained
- 2 medium carrots, grated
- 2 teaspoons minced garlic
- 2 teaspoons chopped fresh basil
- 1 tablespoon nutritional food yeast

Place the cashews, tahini, water, and soy sauce in a food processor and grind into a paste. Add the pimentos, carrots, garlic, basil, and yeast. Process this until smooth. Cashew Cheese will keep in the fridge for up to 1 week.

TWO-CHILE SALSA

This is another recipe that Robin Burnside brought with her when she was head of the Esalen kitchen. It's a flavorful salsa that has a crisp, spicy chile taste. It uses jalapeno, which is a small, green, spicy chile that takes it name from Jalapa, a city in Mexico, and serrano, a flavorful small, green chile that packs a lot of heat. Both of these chiles are common in Mexican salsas.

2 large, fresh, ripe tomatoes
1 small red onion, cut in $1/4$-inch dice
1 fresh jalapeno chile
1 fresh serrano chile
1 tablespoon minced garlic
$1/2$ cup chopped fresh cilantro
1 tablespoon fresh lime juice
$1/2$ teaspoon cumin seed
$1/2$ teaspoon sea salt

LESS SPICY VERSION

To make a less spicy salsa, mince only $1/2$ of the jalapeno chile and eliminate the serrano chile.

Before dicing the tomatoes, cut them in half and scoop out and discard the seeds. Then continue to chop into 1/4-inch dice. Dice the onion and add it to the tomatoes. Slice the jalapeno and the serrano chile down the center lengthwise. Remove the seeds and membrane and discard. Then mince the chiles as fine as you possibly can. Add to the tomatoes along with the garlic, cilantro, and lime juice.

Place the cumin seed in a small fry pan and roast over medium-high heat until the seeds have an aromatic smell and are lightly toasted. Then ground the toasted seed to a fine powder in a seed grinder. Mix the cumin and salt with the other ingredients in a bowl and let the salsa sit for at least 20 minutes to allow the release and build up of flavor.

At Esalen, we serve this salsa with a big bowl of tortilla chips.

RANCHERO SAUCE

This is a Santa Fe version of the recipe also known as Colorado Sauce. The authentic recipe has you prepare the dried chile pods from scratch. If time doesn't allow for this, you can substitute 3/4-cup ground red chile. Be sure to use ground red chile, not chili powder. Denise Ladwig brought this recipe to the Esalen kitchen.

¹/₂	pound dry New Mexico, Arbol, or Anaheim red chile pods
3	quarts chicken stock, vegetable stock, or water from cooked chile pods
4	medium yellow onions, cut in ¹/₂-inch dice
¹/₂	cup olive oil
6–8	cloves garlic, minced
2¹/₂	teaspoons cumin seed
3	teaspoons sea salt

Remove stem and seeds from the dry chiles. Don't worry about getting every seed out as any you miss will sink to the bottom of the pot. Fill a 4-quart saucepan with the stock or water and the chiles. Bring to a boil, and then cover and simmer for about 2 hours or until chiles are tender. Drain chiles in a colander, saving the liquid.

In a skillet over medium heat, sauté onion in olive oil for about 10 minutes or until browned; then add minced garlic and sauté for about 1 minute more.

Dry-roast the cumin seeds in a skillet over medium heat until the seeds have a beautiful aroma (about 2 to 3 minutes). Then grind in a seed grinder.

In a blender or food processor, puree the chiles with the onions, ground cumin, and salt. Add the cooking liquid until the puree is the desired consistency, similar to thick gravy. Much of the spicy heat from the chiles will come from the stock the chiles were cooked in, so taste the sauce periodically as you add the liquid. If you want a really hot sauce, use only the cooking liquid; if a milder sauce is desired, use more plain chicken stock, vegetable stock, or water to thin the puree.

Ranchero Sauce can be used for enchiladas, tamales, huevos rancheros, or burritos. It can also be added to soups like posole (hominy soup) or bean chili.

ROASTED RED PEPPER HUMMUS

A popular lunch at the Esalen dining lodge is the Greek Feast. We serve a Greek salad with freshly picked spinach from the Esalen organic garden and, as an accompaniment, hummus. Hummus is an ancient dish that is popular all over the eastern Mediterranean. Its two main ingredients, chickpeas and sesame seeds, have been cultivated in this part of the world for over five thousand years. This variation adds the sweetness of roasted red pepper blended into the earthy flavors of the hummus.

Makes 3 cups

- 1 roasted red bell pepper
- 1 pound cooked chickpeas (or one 15-ounce can)
- 1/4 cup olive oil
- 2 tablespoons lemon juice
- 1 tablespoon minced garlic
- 1/3 cup tahini (sesame seed butter)
  Pinch cayenne pepper
- 1/2 teaspoon sea salt
- 1/4 cup water from cooking the chickpeas (or vegetable stock)

Roast the bell pepper by placing it over an open flame or in the oven at 450 degrees F. When the skin of the pepper is blackened, place the pepper in a paper bag and seal for about 15 minutes, letting it steam in the bag. Remove it from the bag and peel off the charred skin. Cut it in half and remove the seeds and white veins. Puree the pepper in a food processor.

Add the chickpeas and olive oil to the pureed pepper and process until smooth. Then add the lemon juice, garlic, tahini, cayenne, and salt; process until smooth. Thin the hummus with reserved cooking water or stock if necessary.

ALTERNATE METHOD

If you don't have a food processor, mash the roasted bell pepper with a fork until it is as smooth as possible; then add the cooked chickpeas and mash with a potato masher until it is as smooth as possible. Blend together the oil, lemon juice, and tahini and add to the chickpeas. Again, mash and whisk the mixture to get it as smooth as possible. Then add remaining ingredients.

DESSERTS

Maple-Pecan Apple Crumb Pie | 185

German Chocolate Mousse | 187

Chocolate Tantric Pie | 189

Chocolate Wacky Cake | 190

Johnny's Cheesecake | 192

Panforte | 195

Walnut–Chocolate Chip Cookies | 196

Chocolate-Dipped Coconut Macaroons | 199

Irish Brownies (aka Kongo Bars) | 200

Lemon Poppy Seed Cake | 201

Flourless Almond Torte | 202

Maple-Pecan Apple Crumb Pie

MAPLE-PECAN
APPLE CRUMB PIE

This is an excellent apple pie recipe from a master pie baker. Robin Burnside brought this recipe to the Esalen kitchen along with a long list of other great pies. Robin teaches the pie-making workshop at Esalen—if you want to learn pie making from a master, sign up for one of her courses.

Serves 8

PIECRUST

1	cup whole wheat pastry flour
1¼	cups unbleached all-purpose flour
¼	teaspoon sea salt
2	tablespoons Sucanat (dehydrated cane juice)
1	cup cold unsalted butter
½	cup ice-cold water

To make the piecrust: The best way to mix the flour and butter for pie dough is with a food processor. Place the flours, salt, and Sucanat in a food processor and pulse the mixture. Cut the cold butter in small chunks and pulse it into the flour until you have a texture like coarse bread crumbs. Remove mixture from food processor and place in a mixing bowl to finish. (If you don't have a food processor, place the dry ingredients in a mixing bowl and work the cold butter into the dry ingredients with your fingers or with a pastry cutter. Do this step quickly so the butter doesn't get warm.)

Sprinkle half the ice water over the dough; work dough with your hand by folding and pressing it against the sides of the bowl. Add half again the remaining water and work the dough with your hands, folding and pressing. If the dough has not come together and taken shape, add the remaining ice water and work the dough as you have been doing. The dough should be a little wet to the touch. Wrap it in plastic wrap and refrigerate for 1/2 hour.

After the dough has chilled, roll it out on a lightly floured surface or between 2 pieces of parchment paper. Press dough out with your hands into a 4-inch circle. Then roll out into a 12-inch diameter circle with a rolling pin, rolling from the center outward. Lay the dough evenly over a pie pan and gently lift up the edges of the dough so it slips into the creases of the pan. With your fingers, gently press dough to the sides of the pan. Trim excess, leaving 3/4 inch hanging over the edge of the pan. Turn the edge of the dough under so that it is flush with the edge of the pan. Make a fluted edge by pushing the edge one direction with your index finger and in the opposite direction with the other index finger and thumb. This recipe makes one 10-inch piecrust (or one 9-inch piecrust with a little dough left over).

Robin Burnside

CHOOSING APPLES

When choosing apples for a pie, I recommend using half tart apples, such as Cox Pippen, Gravenstein, or Granny Smith, and half flavorful sweet apples, such as Fuji, Golden, or Johnnygold. The tart apple will hold its shape and bake well, while the sweet apple will cook down into a sauce texture and help develop the flavor of the pie.

PIE FILLING

    6 cups cored, peeled, and sliced apples (about 2$\frac{1}{2}$ pounds cut into $\frac{1}{4}$-inch slices; if using organic apples, leave the skin on)
    2 tablespoons freshly squeezed lemon juice
$\frac{1}{4}$ cup Sucanat (dehydrated cane juice) or honey
    2 teaspoons cinnamon
    2 tablespoons unbleached all-purpose flour
$\frac{1}{3}$ cup maple syrup

To make the filling: In a mixing bowl, mix sliced apples with the lemon juice, and then add the Sucanat or honey, cinnamon, and flour and toss. Add the maple syrup and coat the apples well. Pour apples into unbaked piecrust. The apple filling should appear to be over the edge of the pie pan. Press mixture with a spatula to ensure there are no air pockets.

Cover the filling with Maple-Pecan Crumb Topping and bake in a preheated oven at 400 degrees F for 10 minutes; then reduce heat to 350 degrees F and bake for 50 minutes more or until the apples are tender. Let pie fully cool so its juices will set up before serving.

MAPLE-PECAN CRUMB TOPPING

    4 tablespoons unsalted butter
$\frac{1}{3}$ cup whole wheat pastry flour
$\frac{1}{4}$ cup Sucanat (dehydrated cane juice)
$\frac{1}{3}$ cup rolled oats
    1 teaspoon cinnamon
    3 tablespoons maple syrup
$\frac{1}{2}$ cup chopped pecans

To make the crumb topping: Soften the butter to room temperature, and then place it in a mixing bowl with the flour and Sucanat and blend. Add the oats and cinnamon; mix well. Add the maple syrup and pecans. This should be a crumbly paste.

GERMAN CHOCOLATE MOUSSE

Marion Cascio brought this recipe to Esalen from her parents' restaurant near Hanover, Germany. She worked in the restaurant from the time she was a young girl until she entered culinary school. When we let this "mousse loose" in the dining lodge, it creates havoc, as people can't stop eating it until it's all gone. When we take the empty serving bowl to the dishwashing station, there are even those who follow the bowl to lick it clean!

Serves 6

> 2 cups semisweet chocolate chips
> 4 eggs
> 1 pint whipping cream

In a double boiler, melt the chocolate chips over medium heat, stirring occasionally with a wooden spoon.

In a separate mixing bowl, whisk the eggs thoroughly. When the chocolate is melted, remove from heat and slowly pour eggs into the hot liquid chocolate as you vigorously whisk the mixture with an electric hand mixer or wire whisk. Be sure to pour slowly as you whisk, or you risk the eggs curdling and lumping in the chocolate.

Beat the cream until you have stiff peaks, and then gently fold whipped cream into chocolate mixture. Pour into individual serving bowls and chill in the refrigerator for at least 4 hours before serving.

Chocolate Tantric Pie

CHOCOLATE TANTRIC PIE

This is a sweet chocolate pie with the spicy bite of ginger and cayenne pepper. It's guaranteed to satisfy your sweet tooth, internally warm your belly, and give you that unmistakable tantric glow. There is very little work to creating this dessert. It's a big favorite in the Esalen dining lodge.

Serves 8

1¹/₂ cups half-and-half or whipping cream
   3 cups semisweet chocolate chips
   1 cup chopped almonds
   1 cup chopped candied ginger
 ¹/₂ teaspoon cayenne pepper (optional)
    Piecrust for a 9-inch pie (see page 185)

Over medium heat, bring half-and-half or whipping cream to a simmer in a 1-quart saucepan, stirring to prevent scorching on the bottom. Whisk as you slowly pour the chocolate chips into the cream and continue to stir until the chocolate has melted. Stir in half the almonds and half the ginger. Stir in cayenne if using. Pour mixture into a prebaked 9-inch pie shell. Sprinkle the remaining almonds and ginger on top. Cool until firm, slice, and serve.

CHOCOLATE WACKY CAKE

If you've dined at Esalen in the past six years, chances are you've had this vegan dessert. It's probably one of the most-served desserts to come out of the Esalen bakery. Most diners don't realize that it's vegan (made without animal products) because of its rich texture and taste.

Serves 12

- 5 cups unbleached all-purpose flour
- 3 cups Sucanat (dehydrated cane juice) or brown sugar
- 1 tablespoon baking soda
- 1¹/₂ teaspoons salt
- ²/₃ cup cocoa
- 1 cup vegetable oil
- 3 tablespoons apple cider vinegar
- 3 cups water

In a mixing bowl, sift all the dry ingredients together. In a separate bowl, whisk all the wet ingredients until they are well blended. Add the wet ingredients to the dry; stir just until the ingredients are mixed. Don't overmix.

Pour into two 10-inch round cake pans that have been greased and floured. Bake in a preheated oven at 325 degrees F for about 25 minutes or until a knife inserted in the center comes out clean. Place on a rack to cool. Frost with your favorite frosting.

John Blunt

JOHNNY'S CHEESECAKE

When I was kitchen manager at Esalen, people would come to me and pay to have this cheesecake served to all the diners on their birthday. The recipe came from Johnny's Swedish grandmother and Johnny made it for many of the Carmel and Big Sur restaurants where he worked before arriving at Esalen.

Serves 12

GRAHAM CRACKER CRUST

14 graham crackers
$1/8$ teaspoon sea salt
4 tablespoons unsalted butter

To make the crust: Grind the graham crackers in a food processor for about 1 minute; add the salt and pulse for a few seconds more. You should have about $1 1/2$ cups of crumbs. Melt the butter and with the food processor running, slowly pour in the butter. The crust should hold together when pressed in your hand.

Put crumbs into a buttered springform pie pan. Using the bottom of a drinking glass or measuring cup, press the crust into the pan. This recipe will fill a 6-inch springform to the top, or an 8-inch springform halfway up the sides.

FILLING

16 ounces cream cheese
1 cup sour cream
2 eggs
$1 1/2$ tablespoons freshly squeezed lemon juice
$1/4$ teaspoon salt
5 tablespoons powdered sugar

To make the filling: Mix the cream cheese and sour cream together in a bowl. Blend in the eggs, one at a time, until incorporated. Then add the lemon juice, salt, and powdered sugar. Mix until the filling is velvety and fluffy, which should take about 8 to 10 minutes with an electric mixer.

Pour filling into crust and bake in a preheated oven at 300 degrees F for 45 minutes. The cheesecake should start to brown around the edges and have a slight wiggle in the center when gently shaken. If the cake is overbaked, it will dry and start to crack on top. Remove from oven and let cool. After it is cool, place the cheesecake into the fridge to set up. The cake should be refrigerated for 2 hours before frosting and 8 hours total to firmly set up. It is important to thoroughly chill this dessert. If you cut it before it's completely cool, it will not hold its shape.

FROSTING

- 4 ounces cream cheese
- 1/4 cup sour cream
- 1/4 cup powdered sugar
- 2 tablespoons freshly squeezed lemon juice

To make the frosting: Blend cream cheese and sour cream in a mixing bowl. Add powdered sugar and lemon juice and mix for 5 minutes until the frosting is smooth and has a nice shine. After the cheesecake has cooled for 2 hours, pour frosting onto cake and smooth with a spatula. Cool in the fridge for an additional 6 hours to set.

Panforte

PANFORTE

Flanagan Mackenzie, a half-Irish and half-Italian Esalen baker, discovered this recipe while studying art in Tuscany. She adapted this fruit-and-nut dessert to fit the Esalen crowd. This Tuscan treat has no eggs or sugar.

Serves 12

- 1 cup water
- 3/4 cup maple syrup
- 3/4 cup vegetable oil
- 1 teaspoon cinnamon
- 1/2 teaspoon allspice
- 1/2 teaspoon nutmeg
- 1/2 teaspoon salt
- 2 cups Thompson raisins
- 2 cups unbleached all-purpose flour
- 1 teaspoon baking powder
- 1 teaspoon baking soda
- 2 cups whole shelled almonds
- Powdered sugar for dusting

In a saucepan, mix the water, syrup, and oil, and then whisk in the raisins, spices, and salt. It's okay if the spices don't mix well at first—they will in the end. Bring ingredients to a simmer and let cook for 3 minutes.

In the meantime, sift into a large mixing bowl the flour, baking powder, baking soda, and then stir in almonds. Once the dry ingredients are mixed, pour in the liquid ingredients from the saucepan. Stir with a wooden spoon until mixed, but don't overmix.

Press the mixture into an oiled 9-inch cake pan and bake in a preheated oven at 350 degrees F for 45 minutes. The panforte will come out tender but will not be much higher than when it went in. Cut into 1- x 3-inch fingers and dust with powdered sugar.

WALNUT–CHOCOLATE CHIP COOKIES

These chunky cookies have a chewy texture with walnuts and chocolate chips enrobed in rich chocolate cookie dough.

Makes 2 dozen cookies

1	cup whole wheat flour
1^1/$_2$	cups unbleached all-purpose flour
^{1}/$_2$	cup unsweetened cocoa powder
^{1}/$_2$	teaspoon baking soda
^{1}/$_2$	teaspoon sea salt
1	cup softened, unsalted butter
1^1/$_2$	cups Sucanat (dehydrated cane juice)
3	eggs
1^1/$_2$	cups semisweet chocolate chips
1	cup chopped walnuts

Work scholar with India Hunt-Bedina and Ashley Smith

In a mixing bowl, sift the flours, cocoa, soda, and salt, and then mix well. In another mixing bowl, mix the butter and Sucanat until blended, and then add the eggs and whisk until the mixture is light and fluffy. Stir in the flour mixture, and then add the chocolate chips and walnuts, stirring just until mixed. Do not overmix.

Cover a baking sheet with parchment paper and spoon cookie dough onto it by heaping tablespoons. Bake in a preheated oven at 350 degrees F for 20 minutes. Remove baking sheet from oven and place on a wire rack to cool. For a chewy cookie, take them out of the oven when they are a little soft to the touch.

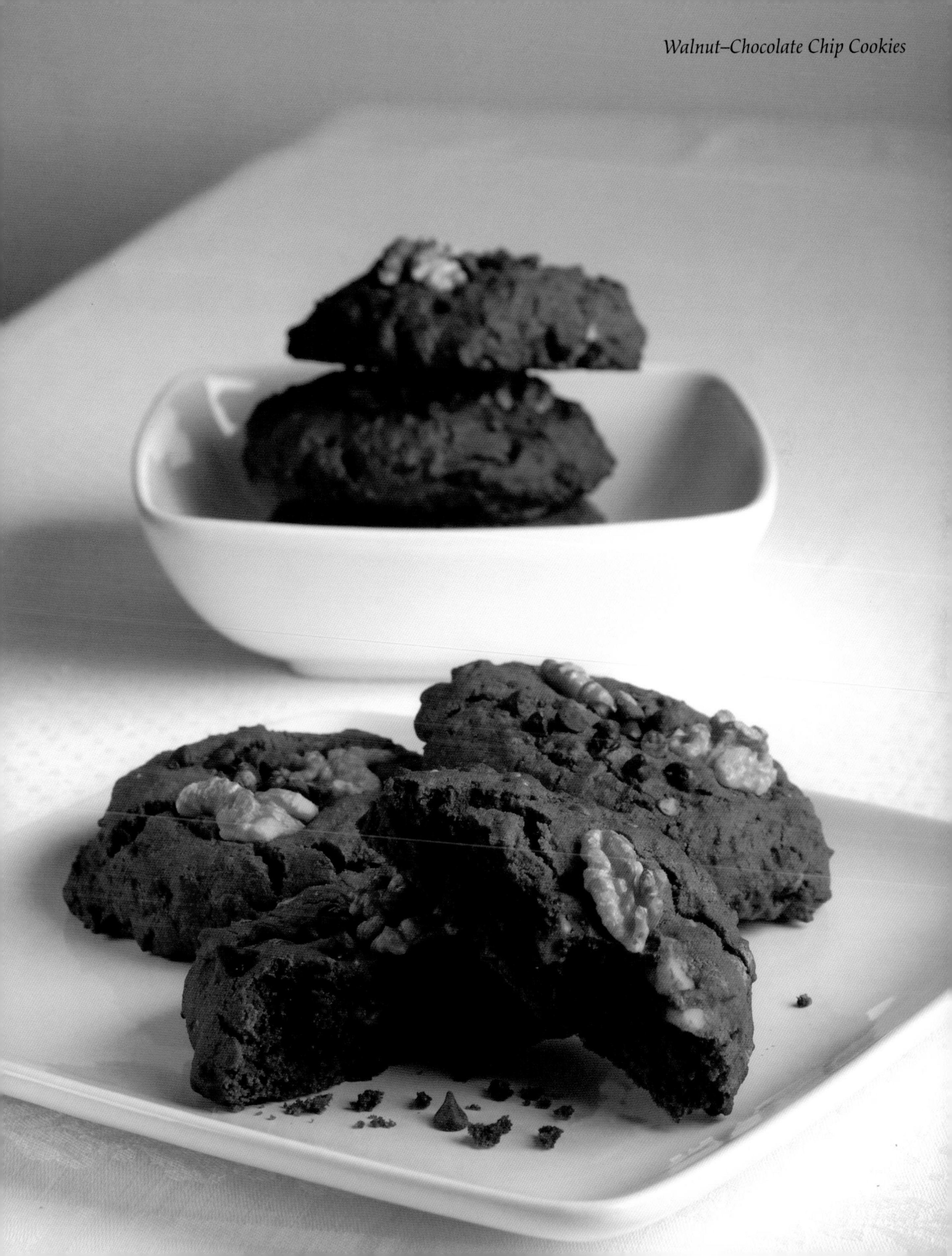

Walnut–Chocolate Chip Cookies

CHOCOLATE-DIPPED COCONUT MACAROONS

Bill Schrier, who left a job as a federal attorney to spend a year in the Esalen kitchen, perfected this classic macaroon recipe. Although Bill had never professionally done it before, he wanted to bake and cook. We were pleasantly surprised when we discovered that he had a hidden talent for it. This is one of his recipes that will always be remembered.

Makes 12 2-inch macaroons

MACAROONS

- 6 egg whites
- 1 teaspoon vanilla
- ¼ cup unbleached all-purpose flour
- 1 cup Sucanat (dehydrated cane juice) or brown sugar
- 4 cups finely shredded coconut

CHOCOLATE DIP

- 2 cups semisweet chocolate chips
- 2 tablespoons unsalted butter

To make the macaroons: Separate the eggs and place the egg whites in a mixing bowl. Using a hand mixer or whisk, beat whites until they are stiff. Continue to beat and add in the vanilla, flour, and Sucanat. Gently fold in the coconut and mix well. The dough will be sticky.

Using an ice cream scoop (or by heaping tablespoons), drop the dough into little domes about 2 inches in diameter on a lightly oiled or parchment-covered baking sheet. Space domes about 1 inch apart. Bake in a preheated oven at 375 degrees F for about 15 minutes or until the macaroons turn a light golden brown. Remove from oven and let cool for 3 minutes so the cookies can set. Then with a spatula, place cookies on a wire rack. These cookies are great with or without the chocolate dip.

To make the chocolate dip: Let the macaroons cool for 45 minutes. Meanwhile, place a saucepan with a small amount of water over low heat and put a smaller metal bowl inside the saucepan. The metal bowl should sit tightly on edge of the pan and not touch the water. Melt the butter; then pour in the chocolate chips and stir occasionally until the chocolate is melted and smooth. Remove from heat.

Holding each cookie by the top of the dome, place the bottom of it into the melted chocolate and dip until chocolate goes up the sides a bit. When finished dipping, if any melted chocolate is left over, it can be dribbled over the tops of the macaroons. Place dipped cookies on a tray or plate that has been covered with parchment paper. Put in the fridge for about 10 minutes until chocolate has set or leave at room temperature until the chocolate is firm.

IRISH BROWNIES
(AKA KONGO BARS)

This is a recipe that our Irish chef Liam brought to the Esalen bakery. It's been in his family for generations and he can't remember where it originated. He has fond boyhood memories of his mother teaching him this recipe. This was the first dessert that he baked. Little did he know that this recipe would be the start of a lifelong profession?

Serves 12

Liam McDermott

- 2 cups packed brown sugar
- 2/3 cup vegetable oil
- 3 eggs
- 2 teaspoons vanilla
- 2 cups unbleached all-purpose flour
- 1 tablespoon non-aluminum baking powder
- 1/2 teaspoon salt
- 3/4 cup chocolate chips

In a mixing bowl, blend the brown sugar and oil, and then add the eggs one at a time until incorporated. Don't overmix. Add vanilla.

Sift the flour, baking powder, and salt into another mixing bowl. Stir the dry ingredients into the sugar mixture until mixed, and then add the chocolate chips and stir until blended.

Pour batter into an oiled 9- x 12-inch baking pan and bake in a preheated oven at 350 degrees F for about 30 minutes or until a knife inserted into the bars comes out clean. Cool and cut into 12 squares.

LEMON POPPY SEED CAKE

Both poppy seeds and lemons have been used in cooking since ancient times. The poppy seed came from the Middle East and the lemon originated in Southeast Asia. This cake has been enjoyed at Esalen by our guests for years. It's a recipe that is one of the basics that every new Esalen baker learns in his or her training.

Serves 10 to 12

- 2 cups Sucanat (dehydrated cane juice) or brown sugar
- 1½ cups vegetable oil
- 4 eggs
- 1 cup milk
- 2 teaspoons lemon extract
- 3 cups unbleached all-purpose flour
- 1 teaspoon baking soda
- ½ teaspoon sea salt
- 2 tablespoons fresh lemon zest
- 1 cup poppy seeds
  Lemon Glaze (see sidebar)

Place the Sucanat or brown sugar in a mixing bowl and slowly pour in the oil, whisking or stirring vigorously as you pour. Beat the eggs into this mixture one at a time. Add the milk and lemon extract and beat until smooth.

In a separate bowl, sift the flour, baking soda, and salt together, and then gently stir this into the liquid mixture until it is completely incorporated. Fold in the lemon zest and poppy seeds, and then pour batter into a well-greased and floured cake pan. At Esalen we use a loaf pan for this recipe, but my preference is a 9-inch Bundt pan.

Place cake in an oven that has been preheated to 325 degrees F and bake for 1 hour or until a knife inserted into the cake comes out clean. Place cake on a wire rack to cool; then top with Lemon Glaze.

LEMON GLAZE

- ½ cup freshly squeezed lemon juice
- 10 tablespoons powdered sugar
- 1 tablespoon fresh lemon zest

Stir all of the ingredients together a small saucepan over medium-high and bring to a boil. Lower the heat to low and let the glaze simmer for 10 minutes. Remove from heat and let cool for 5 minutes, and then pour over the cooled cake. The glaze should soak into the cake.

Charlie Cascio

ALMOND MEAL

Most food processors can't grind almonds fine enough for this recipe, although it's possible to use a food processor as long as you have a very sharp chopping blade (the S-shaped blade). What I've found that works best for this recipe is a little seed grinder (sometimes called an electric coffee grinder). It takes about 1/2 pound of almonds to make 2 cups of almond meal. By grinding small quantities of almonds in batches, the task can be completed quickly.

FLOURLESS ALMOND TORTE

I think this is a wonderful cake. It's so wonderful that I ordered it for my wedding cake. My predecessor, Robin Burnside, brought it to the Esalen bakery. It's a light, moist cake with a superb almond flavor that won me over with my first bite. Robin is a great baker and chef, and she ran the Esalen kitchen for five years before retiring the post to me.

Serves 12

6 fresh eggs
$1/2$ teaspoon cream of tartar
$1/3$ cup sweetener (sugar, maple syrup, or honey*)
$1/2$ teaspoon vanilla
$1/2$ teaspoon almond extract
2 cups almond meal (see sidebar)

If using honey, use only $1/4$ cup.

Separate the whites from the yolks of the eggs. Place whites with cream of tartar in a mixing bowl and beat until stiff, but not dry. Gently fold in the sweetener of your choice. Do this slowly so you do not break down the bubbles in the egg whites. Beat the egg yolks and slowly fold them into the mixture as gently as possible. Add vanilla and almond extract. Sprinkle the ground almonds gently into the mixture as you fold to incorporate.

A 10-inch springform pan works best with this torte, but any cake pan will do. Lightly oil the bottom only of the pan or line with parchment paper. The torte bakes best when it clings to the sides of the pan. Gently pour the mixture into the pan. Bake in an oven preheated to 350 degrees F for about 30 minutes or until a knife inserted in the torte comes out clean. Remove pan from oven and gently slip a knife around the sides of the pan before releasing the springform. Serve with fresh whipped cream and sun-ripened raspberries or your favorite summer fruit.

INDEX